The Science of

NATURAL

DISASTERS

⚠ When Nature and Humans Collide ⚠

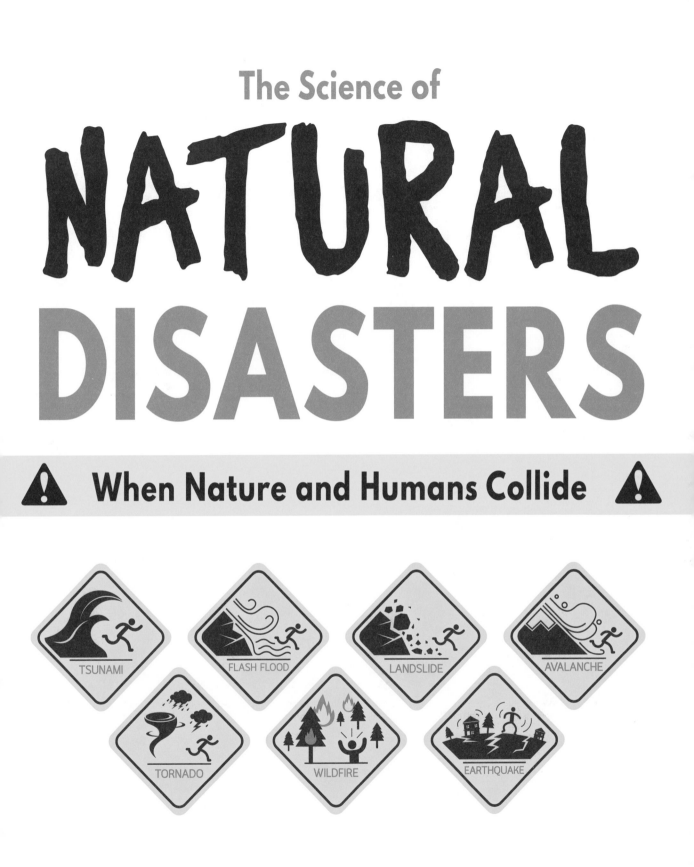

DIANE C. TAYLOR

Illustrated by Traci Van Wagoner

Nomad Press

A division of Nomad Communications

10 9 8 7 6 5 4 3 2 1

This book was manufactured by Versa Press, East Peoria, Illinois
January 2020, Job #J19-10195
ISBN Softcover: 978-1-61930-858-9
ISBN Hardcover: 978-1-61930-855-8

Educational Consultant, Marla Conn

Questions regarding the ordering of this book should be addressed to
Nomad Press
2456 Christian St., White River Junction, VT 05001
www.nomadpress.net

Printed in the United States.

Titles in the Inquire & Investigate
Earth Science set

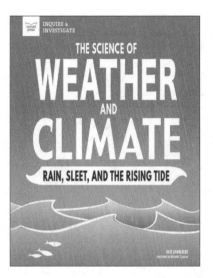

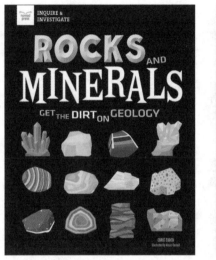

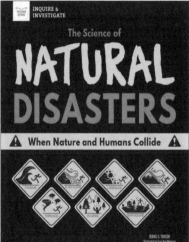

You can use a smartphone or tablet app to scan the QR codes and explore more! Cover up neighboring QR codes to make sure you're scanning the right one. You can find a list of URLs on the Resources page.

If the QR code doesn't work, try searching the internet with the Keyword Prompts to find other helpful sources.

Interested in primary sources? Look for this icon.

🔍 natural disasters

What are source notes?

In this book, you'll find small numbers at the end of some paragraphs. These numbers indicate that you can find source notes for that section in the back of the book. Source notes tell readers where the writer got their information. This might be a news article, a book, or another kind of media. Source notes are a way to know that what you are reading is information that other people have verified. They can also lead you to more places where you can explore a topic that you're curious about!

Contents

TIMELINE

1650 BCE .... The volcanic eruption on the island of Santorini in Greece produces 7 cubic miles of magma and releases enough ash into the air to contribute to the end of the Minoan culture on the island of Crete.

August 24, 79 CE .... The volcanic eruption of Mount Vesuvius destroys the Roman cities of Pompeii and Herculaneum.

132 CE .... Chinese astronomer and mathematician Chang Heng (78–139) invents the first seismograph, known as the Dragon Jar.

365 CE .... An undersea earthquake with an epicenter near the island of Crete causes destruction in Greece, Libya, Egypt, Cyprus, and Sicily. A resulting tsunami kills thousands along the eastern coast of the Mediterranean Sea.

May 20–29, 526 CE .... The Antioch earthquake in Syria crumbles buildings and sets off a series of fires that destroy the buildings left standing. It claims an estimated 250,000 lives.

October, 11, 1138 .... One of the largest earthquakes in ancient human history takes place in Aleppo, Syria, claiming the lives of more than 200,000 people.

May 20, 1202 .... An earthquake near Syria may have led to the deaths of as many as 1 million people.

January 23, 1556 .... An earthquake in the area of Shaanxi, China, rocks the land and affects the lives of millions of people and kills an estimated 830,000.

November 1, 1755 .... An earthquake in Lisbon, Portugal, opens a fissure 16 feet wide in the center of the city and creates a tsunami that roars through the town.

November 25, 1839 .... The port village of Coringa, India, is destroyed by the strong winds of a hurricane and a resulting storm surge that reaches a height of 40 feet.

1870 .... U.S. President Ulysses S. Grant (1822–1885) establishes the National Weather Service to monitor weather on a daily basis and warn people of hazardous weather conditions, such as hurricanes and heavy rains.

1880 .... British geologist John Milne (1850–1913) invents the first modern seismograph, which consists of a horizontal pendulum.

May–August, 1883 .... The volcanic island of Krakatoa, in Indonesia, explodes, creating the loudest sound ever recorded on Earth and causing two catastrophic tsunamis.

TIMELINE

1896................................ French meteorologist Leon Teisserenc de Bort (1855–1913), using hundreds of weather balloons in experiments, discovers that Earth's atmosphere is made up of different layers.

September 8–9, 1900........ The Great Galveston hurricane inundates the town of Galveston, Texas, with a storm surge that floods the entire island. When the storm ends, nothing remains standing in an area covering nearly 2,000 acres.

1912................................ German geologist Alfred Wegener (1880–1930) proposes that the continents were once a single landmass and that they have been, and still are, drifting apart.

March 18, 1925 .... The Tri-State Tornado cuts a path 219 miles long through Missouri, Illinois, and Indiana. The tornado lasts a record-breaking three-and-a-half hours and claims the lives of 695 people.

July–November, 1931........ Years of drought followed by a harsh winter create the conditions for catastrophic flooding on major rivers in eastern and central China. Subsequent epidemics and famine result in one of the worst natural disasters of the twentieth century.

January 13, 1939.............. The state of Victoria, Australia, is overwhelmed by a series of wildfires that burn nearly 5 million acres of land. The Black Friday Bushfires completely destroy five towns and damage 16 others.

1968................................ Recognizing that fire is a natural process crucial to the health of ecosystems, the National Park Service of the United States changes its policy regarding wildfires. Previously, all wildfires had been put out as soon as possible. Now, they are allowed to burn, provided they do not run out of control.

December 26, 2004.......... An earthquake in the Indian Ocean creates a tsunami that washes over coastal communities all across the Indian Ocean. Countries affected include South Africa, Tanzania, Kenya, India, Myanmar, Indonesia, Thailand, and Malaysia. More than 220,000 people lose their lives in the disaster.

August 23–31, 2005.......... A Category 5 storm named Hurricane Katrina cuts a path of devastation all the way from Cuba to Canada. Hardest hit is New Orleans, Louisiana, where a storm surge leads to 53 levee breaches. Strong winds blow out the windows of high-rise hotels and toss beds into the air. Thousands of people flee their homes only to wind up stranded in deplorable conditions at the city's covered sports stadium.

July–November, 2018........ Wildfire season in California sparks 8,527 fires. The fires burn 1,893,913 acres of land, cause more than $3 billion in property damage, and kill 96 civilians and six firefighters.

Introduction
Warning!

What is a natural disaster?

A natural disaster is an event in nature that causes harm to the human population, such as tornadoes, hurricanes, volcanic eruptions, and many other events.

When humans live in harmony with nature, all is well. Rain falls to water our crops, the sun shines to grow them, rivers flow across the land to provide water and transportation routes. Humans couldn't exist without nature to support us—as a species, we are tied to the cycles of the natural world.

Unfortunately, human beings and nature are not always on the best of terms. Have you ever been in a hurricane, a flood, or a tornado? Have you ever lived someplace that experienced a drought? When a natural event such as these causes significant damage to a human population, we call it a natural disaster.

In 2018, people from all around the globe found themselves in desperate circumstances because of natural disasters. About 27 miles from Guatemala City, Guatemala, a volcano named Mount Fuego erupted without warning on June 3. An ash column soared more than 9 miles into the atmosphere, burying several villages in hot ash and melting car tires into the ground.

Later that month, three people in Rio Grande do Sul, Brazil, were driving on highway RS-463 when a tornado snatched their trucks off the road and tossed them into nearby fields. Two people died, thousands of homes were damaged, and more than 200,000 chickens in 10 different aviaries were killed.

The month of July brought three times the normal amount of rainfall into southwestern Japan. The resulting floods and mudslides claimed the lives of at least 100 people and left 2 million without a place to call home.

July was a tough month for the citizens of California, too. Record high temperatures, dry vegetation, and the misdeeds of an arsonist resulted in 17 active wildfires. They burned along a 650-mile corridor from the north of the state to the south, destroying 300,000 acres of land and more than 600 homes.

VOCAB LAB

There is a lot of new vocabulary in this book. Turn to the glossary in the back when you come to a word you don't understand. Practice your new vocabulary in the VOCAB LAB activities in each chapter.

An aerial view of Mount Fuego in Guatemala and the wide range of likely damage its eruption caused, shown by the areas of red and yellow

credit: NASA/JPL-Caltech/ESA/Copernicus/Google

In late September, more than 2,000 people died and another 330,000 were left homeless when a massive earthquake struck the Central Sulawesi province of Indonesia. Then, in early October, people as far south as Central America and as far north as the Atlantic coast of Canada battled the wind, rain, and storm surge of Hurricane Michael. Houses were flattened, hundreds of roads were closed, and more than 3 million acres of timberland were destroyed.

What do all of these events have in common? They are all natural disasters.

THE HUMAN ELEMENT

Natural events have always had profound effects on the organisms that inhabit Earth. Our planet is more than 4 billion years old. During that time, the planet has experienced five mass extinction events, been covered in ice, and turned into a global desert.

Those were certainly extreme events. But we classify a natural disaster as a natural event that has an adverse effect on a human population.

The meteor that struck Earth 65 million years ago, causing the dinosaurs to go extinct, was a catastrophe for dinosaurs, but not for humans. We wouldn't even be on the planet until millions of years later. So, that meteor is not a natural disaster.

Even today, when more than 7 billion humans live on Earth, natural events with the potential of being classified as natural disasters are not always natural disasters. For example, thousands of earthquakes occur around the globe each year, but most of them have no affect on humans.

The biggest hurricane in Earth's history might form in the basin of the Atlantic Ocean, but if it never makes landfall or capsizes a fleet of ships, it will fail to rise to the level of a natural disaster.

A landslide in El Salvador, 2001

credit: United States Geological Survey

CLASSIFYING CALAMITIES

Classifications help answer one of science's most basic questions: What is it? The process of sorting things out and developing a method to accurately group similar things together helps us make sense of a complex physical world.

In the field of earth science, a natural disaster is classified under one of five different headings.

Geological Disasters. Geology is the study of the materials that form our planet and the processes that act upon them. Geological natural disasters include avalanches, landslides, earthquakes, sinkholes, and volcanic eruptions.

Hydrological Disasters. Hydrology is the study of the movement, distribution, and quality of water. Water-related natural disasters include floods, tsunamis, and rare events known as limnic eruptions, which is when carbon dioxide suddenly erupts from deep lake waters and forms a gas cloud.

A limnic eruption takes place when dissolved carbon dioxide (CO_2) erupts from deep within a lake and forms a suffocating gas cloud. This YouTube video investigates the limnic eruption that exploded out of Lake Nyos in Cameroon, Africa, in August 1986. Why are these such rare occurrences?

🔍 limnic eruption sci

SCIENTIFIC METHOD

The scientific method is the process scientists use to ask questions and find answers. Keep a science journal to record your methods and observations during all the activities in this book. You can use a scientific method worksheet to keep your ideas and observations organized.

Question: What are we trying to find out? What problem are we trying to solve?

Research: What is already known about this topic?

Hypothesis: What do we think the answer will be?

Equipment: What supplies are we using?

Method: What procedure are we following?

Results: What happened and why?

The trail left by a meteor above Chelyabinsk, Russia, in 2013

credit: tonynetone (CC BY 2.0)

Meteorological Disasters. Meteorologists forecast the weather by studying the physics and chemistry of the atmosphere. Weather-related natural disasters include blizzards, droughts, thunderstorms, hurricanes, hailstorms, heat waves, and tornadoes.

Space Disasters. When comets, asteroids, or meteors burn up in space, they can cause an explosion that impacts Earth. For example, on February 15, 2013, a large meteor entered Earth's atmosphere over the southwest area of Chelyabinsk, Russia. When the meteor exploded about 18 miles above Earth, it produced a flash of light brighter than the sun, as well as a hot cloud of dust and ash. The brilliance of the meteor's light caused temporary blindness in a number of eyewitnesses. The blast created by the meteor's air burst caused extensive ground damage and blew out the windows in homes.

Wildfire Disasters. Large, destructive fires that begin in grasslands or forests and spread into areas of human habitation occur all over the world. Each year they cause millions of dollars of damage and force thousands of people out of their homes.

RESPONSE TO NATURAL DISASTERS

Since ancient times, human beings have sought to understand the origins of natural disasters. As centuries passed, our efforts have led us from blaming the gods for our earthly misfortunes to blaming ourselves to investigating the fundamental workings of our world.

In the realm of science, our inquiries into such things as why volcanoes erupt, where earthquakes will strike, or when hurricanes will sweep in along our coasts have led to some of the most important earth science discoveries of the modern era.

> Despite our newfound knowledge, however, we have yet to perfect systems that protect us from the severe damage that results from natural disasters.

We have made progress, but much work remains to be done if we are to safeguard ourselves from the most destructive aspects of the natural world.

In *Natural Disasters*, we will examine six of the most destructive natural forces on Earth, exploring the science behind earthquakes, volcanoes, hurricanes, tornadoes, floods, and wildfires. We will also delve into the social history and cultural reactions that have been part of some of the worst natural disasters on Earth.

Ready to learn more about the awesome energy of the natural world? Let's go!

WHAT IS EARTH SCIENCE?

Earth science, or geoscience, explores the physical makeup of Earth and its atmosphere. Scientists who work in earth science might spend a lot of time working outdoors. Back in their labs and offices, earth scientists rely on a combination of physics, chemistry, biology, geography, and chronology to formulate a quantitative understanding of Earth and how it works.

KEY QUESTIONS

- **How does classification promote understanding? Does this work in fields besides science?**

- **Should the definition of natural disasters be expanded to include catastrophic events that cause no harm to humans? Why or why not?**

WHAT DO SCIENTISTS *DO*?

What do geologists, hydrologists, and meteorologists actually do for work? These are the scientists who make discoveries that can affect everyone on the planet, so their jobs are pretty important. Investigate one of their jobs and find out!

- **Head to the library or go online and research the careers of geologist, hydrologist, and meteorologist.** Use the following questions to guide your research.

  - What type of environment would you work in as one of these scientists?

  - How much of your work life would be spent outdoors? How much would be spent inside?

  - What might an average day on the job be like?

  - How much education would you need to become a scientist working in that field?

  - Would you be more likely to find work in a private company or in the government?

  - On average, how much money could you expect to make in a year?

- **Create a written or visual presentation of your findings.** How are these careers different?

> **To investigate more,** contact a working scientist and conduct an interview with them about their job. Is the reality of the profession close to what you discovered through research? Does this sound like a field you might explore as a career?

Chapter 1

Earthquakes: When the Earth Shakes

What causes the
earth to move during
an earthquake?

Enormous shifting landmasses called tectonic plates move in ways that send energy zinging through the earth's crust, causing the ground to shake and sometimes leading to death and destruction on a large scale.

All Saints' Day, November 1, 1755, marked one of the most important religious festival days of the Catholic calendar in Europe. This was especially the case in the prosperous port city of Lisbon, the capital city of Portugal and the fourth-largest city in Europe. Thousands of Catholic residents of Lisbon were attending Mass that morning around the city when a sudden, violent shaking of the earth knocked them off their feet and collapsed the walls of their churches.

A fissure 16 feet wide cracked open in the center of the city. As buildings crumbled around them, residents flocked to the relative safety of the docks, an open space with few tall structures that were likely to collapse.

However, 40 minutes after the shaking began, people watched in horror as a massive wave appeared as if from nowhere and crashed into the Tagus River. Water roared up the channel of the river, overwhelming everything and everyone in its path.

Next came an all-engulfing fire. Inside Lisbon's 40-plus churches and in homes throughout the city, thousands of candles had been lit for the religious holiday. Toppled by the shaking of the earth, the candles set fire to the city. The resulting firestorm was so intense, even people 100 feet away from the blaze suffocated from the heat and toxic air.[1]

Where did the Lisbon earthquake come from? What caused the earth to tremble and tear apart? Why did a mountain of water rise up from the ocean and flood the Tagus River?

To answer these questions, we need to examine the interior of Earth itself, from the surface we walk upon all the way to the core. We also need to explore the complex, dynamic relationships that exist among the world's continents.

OUR TREMBLING PLANET

The U.S. Geological Survey estimates that 12,000 to 14,000 earthquakes occur throughout the world each year. There is always an earthquake shaking the planet somewhere! Most of them are relatively harmless. Minor earthquakes occur several hundred times a day. Major earthquakes occur about once a month. Great earthquakes, such as the one that leveled Lisbon in 1755, occur about once a year.[2]

An illustration showing the tsunami associated with the 1755 earthquake

credit: Arnold Guyot, 1873

From the surface we walk on to the planet's deepest interior, Earth is composed of three main layers of very different materials. The crust forms the outermost layer of Earth and extends from 3 to 45 feet. But not all crust is the same.

- Oceanic crust is the thinnest part of Earth's crust. The material in oceanic crust is made up of dense, heavy rocks, such as basalt.

- Continental crust is the ground that makes up the world's landmasses. It is the thickest part of Earth's crust and is made up of lighter, less dense rocks, such as quartz and granite, than those found in oceanic crust.

The mantle is the thickest part of Earth's interior, extending for more than 1,500 miles. The material in the mantle resembles that of the continental crust, with an important difference. The mantle is hot, warmed internally by heat left over from the original formation of the planet and the decay of radioactive materials such as uranium, thorium, and potassium.

The mantle is solid, but hot enough for the rocks to exist in a plastic state—they are solid but pliable.

The core is the deepest level of our planet. It is divided into a solid inner core and a liquid outer core, believed to be composed primarily of iron and nickel.

What do these layers have to do with earthquakes?

THE DRIFTING CONTINENTS

In your day-to-day experience, the ground beneath your feet seems perfectly stable. In fact, though, the continents you walk upon are constantly moving. Slowly, during the course of a year, North America, South America, Asia, Africa, Antarctica, and Australia move 10 to 40 millimeters. That's about the same rate as the growth of human hair and fingernails.

Look at a map of the world, and imagine the continents as pieces of a puzzle. Do you see how they might be pieced back together to form a single landmass? Turn the continents this way and that, and you can pull them all together to form one continuous stretch of land.

This is exactly what scientists from earlier centuries noticed—the coastlines of the continents looked as if they might once have formed a single landmass. People speculated for years that a single continent, which they named Pangaea, existed millions of years ago. But none of the theories they came up with to explain how the continents moved satisfied the demands of scientific proof. The theory of continental drift remained in doubt.

By the 1960s, however, advances in scientific technology and a deeper understanding of Earth's interior finally settled the question. The continents had moved, they were still moving, and that movement was responsible for the creation of earthquakes.

A map of the world as it exists today

A map of the world as it existed before the continents drifted apart

What geologists clarified in the 1960s was that Earth's crust is divided into an upper and a lower sphere. The upper sphere—called the lithosphere—is solid. The lower sphere—called the asthenosphere—is semi-solid. The continents are part of enormous sections of the lithosphere called tectonic plates, which settle on the surface of the semi-solid asthenosphere. That asthenosphere moves, and as the asthenosphere moves, so do the tectonic plates.

What causes the asthenosphere to move? That question baffled scientists for years! For a long time, the most widely accepted theory was that Earth was shrinking, drying out as if it were an aging apple. As the planet shrank, it deformed, and the continents were pulled apart.

We know now that molten rock is what keeps tectonic plates in motion.

The material our planet is composed of is part of a never-ending cycle. Molten rock bubbles up from deep inside the planet, creating new earth that slowly pushes the continents apart. That same motion also causes entire continents to be slowly pushed back down toward the center of the hot inner core of Earth.

The continents move not because Earth is expanding or contracting, but because the material of the planet is always being recycled. It is the movement created by that recycling that pushes the continents around on the molten surface of the asthenosphere.

DISASTER FACT

The continents make up the seven major tectonic plates. But there are dozens of smaller tectonic plates, as well. They are all in motion, pushing and pulling against one another, creating thousands of earthquakes every year.

The tectonic plates of the world

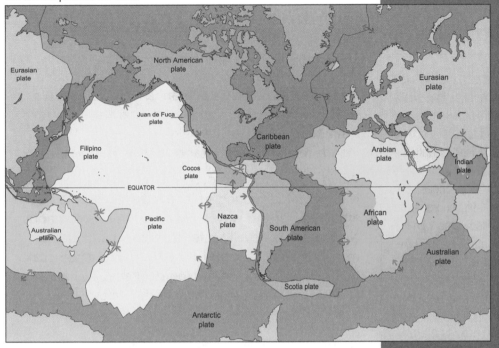

WHOSE FAULT IS IT?

All seismic activity originates in the earth's crust, and all earthquakes are the result of immense pressure building up—and suddenly being released—around the boundaries of tectonic plates. As the continents slowly move, they run up against one another, and they push and pull against one another with terrific force.

Thousands of years might pass with two or more tectonic plates pushing against one another with no resulting earthquake. But, when that pressure does finally break, a tremendous amount of energy might be released as seismic waves. According to the Center for Earthquake Research and Information, a relatively small earthquake is equivalent to an explosion of six tons of TNT. A great earthquake releases as much energy as 99 million tons of TNT—the equivalent of 25,000 nuclear bombs.[3]

SHOCKING EVENTS

The initial eruption of a large earthquake always grabs big headlines. But most major earthquakes are followed by a series of aftershocks as well. These smaller, less destructive earthquakes can last for days, months, or even years after the first big quake. The great earthquake that hit Japan in 2011, for example, produced more than 5,000 aftershocks in the following year alone.

FAULT LINES

The intensity and duration of earthquakes is partially decided by the length and width of the fault line. The longer and wider the fault, the deadlier a major earthquake can be. The longest and widest fault line yet to be recorded came with the 2004 Sumatra earthquake. Registering 9.1 on the MMS, this earthquake was the result of activity on a fault line that was more than 100 miles wide and 900 miles long. The fault ruptured on the floor of the Indian Ocean. The resulting tsunamis were the worst in recorded history, killing an estimated 227,000 people in coastal communities that line the Indian Ocean.

DISASTER FACT

Earthquakes are called seismic events. The word *seismic* is from the Greek words *selen* ("to shake") and *seismos* ("earthquake").

MEASURING THE MAGNITUDE

The strength of an earthquake is determined by the amplitude of seismic waves as they are recorded on devices known as seismographs. A wave has two main characteristics—amplitude and wave length. Amplitude refers to the height of a wave. Wave length refers to the distance between waves.

When an earthquake occurs, geologists assign it a magnitude rating of 1 to 9 based on the amplitude of the waves recorded on seismographs. News reports usually refer to these magnitude measurements as being based on the Richter scale. In 1935, American seismologist Charles Richter (1900–1985) created a magnitude scale that was used for many years.

Most seismologists today, however, base their assessments on a scale known as the Moment Magnitude Scale (MMS). The numbers and magnitudes have stayed the same, but the methods of determining magnitude have improved since the time of Charles Richter.

Amplitude determines the intensity of a wave. The higher the amplitude, the stronger the wave.

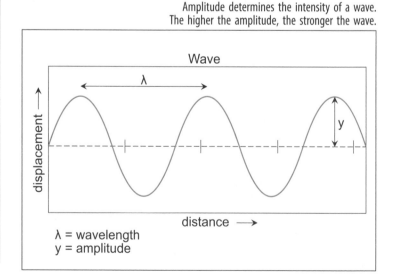

Wave

λ

displacement →

distance →

y

λ = wavelength
y = amplitude

A fissure in a highway after the 1964 Anchorage, Alaska, earthquake

Earthquakes that measure from 1 to 4 on the MMS are rarely cause for alarm. A seismograph may pick up a minor earthquake (1 to 1.9 on the MMS), but the waves will not even be felt by people in the area of the quake. An earthquake with a magnitude rating between 2 and 4 will only rattle some objects in nearby houses.

The time for concern is when an earthquake registers a magnitude between 5 and 9. On the low end of that range, poorly constructed buildings within the area of the quake will be damaged. On the high end of that range, entire cities can be destroyed.

A major earthquake can create untold amounts of destruction in a matter of seconds. Most earthquakes last no more than 10 to 30 seconds. Earthquakes that last longer, from one to five minutes, are extremely rare. But they do happen. On March 27, 1964, for example, an earthquake in Alaska shook the ground for more than four minutes. At a magnitude rating of 9.2, the 1964 Alaska earthquake remains the strongest ever recorded in the United States.

MAKING WAVES

The energy released by an earthquake takes the form of seismic waves. There are two categories of seismic waves, and two types of waves under each category.

- **Body waves** travel through the interior of the earth.

  ○ **Compression waves**, or P waves—the P stands for "primary"—behave just like sound waves, moving particles parallel to the surface of the earth.

  ○ **Shear waves**, or S waves— for "secondary"—move particles perpendicular to the surface of the earth. They travel slower than P waves, but cause more disruption.

- **Surface waves** travel along the surface of Earth.

  ○ **Rayleigh waves** travel in backward rotating circles.

  ○ **Love waves** vibrate perpendicular to the surface. They are the most destructive of all four types of seismic waves.

EARTHQUAKES AND THE LAND

THE RING OF FIRE

Most earthquakes occur in an area that geologists have named the Ring of Fire. The ring is a vast, horseshoe-shaped expanse that covers 25,000 miles on the basin of the Pacific Ocean. The ring is formed by the movement of tectonic plates and accounts for 90 percent of the world's earthquakes. More than 80 percent of the largest earthquakes have taken place within the Ring of Fire.

The Ring of Fire

All earthquakes cause some disruption of Earth's crust. In a minor earthquake, the shaking may be so minimal we don't even know an earthquake has occurred. When major or great earthquakes strike, however, the damage to land is impossible to miss.

We saw how an enormous fissure opened up in the center of Lisbon during a major earthquake in 1755. But earthquakes can disrupt the land in other dramatic ways as well.

When one tectonic plate suddenly slips underneath another, for example, huge portions of land may be uplifted or subsided, which means they are lowered. Such events change the shape of the land. A 2016 earthquake on New Zealand's South Island, for example, lifted the seabed along the coast of Kaikoura from 2 to 18 feet. Marine creatures were left high and dry as they suddenly found themselves on a raised platform high above sea level.

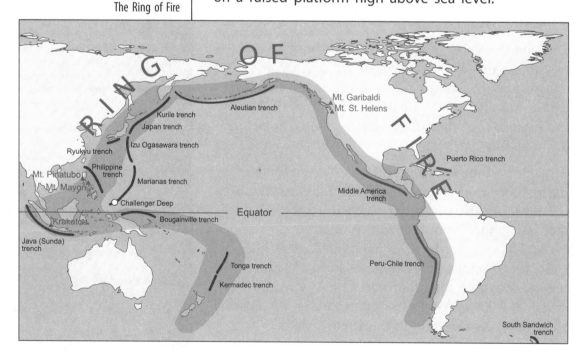

Eyewitnesses to the disaster did not comment on the shaking of the earth as much as they did on the sound of massive amounts of water pouring off the newly uplifted land.

Can you imagine what that
might have been like?

Earthquakes can also create landslides and avalanches and, when soil conditions are right, the shaking of an earthquake can make partially saturated soil behave as if it were a liquid. The process is called soil liquefaction and it can cause enormous amounts of destruction. In the 2018 earthquake in the Central Sulawesi province of Indonesia, soil liquefaction buried two villages under 9 feet of mud, turning them into mass graves.

During an earthquake in Mexico City, Mexico, in 1985, buildings constructed on soft soil suffered severe damage.

You can see some of the devastation wrought by the 2016 New Zealand earthquake in this aerial footage.

Guardian
Kaikoura
video

THE PARTS OF AN EARTHQUAKE

There are five major parts of an earthquake. The point where an earthquake originates is called the focus, or hypocenter. Seismic waves radiate in all directions from the focus of an earthquake. The point on the surface of the earth located directly above the focus is called the epicenter. The fault plane is the flat surface along which there is a slip between tectonic plates during an earthquake. A fault line is a fracture in the earth's crust as a result of an earthquake.

EARTHQUAKES AND TSUNAMIS

THE 2011 JAPANESE EARTHQUAKE

In 2011, Japan experienced the strongest earthquake in the country's history and the fourth-strongest earthquake in the world since the use of modern seismography. The epicenter of the earthquake was located about 40 miles east of the Oshika Peninsula. The quake's hypocenter was located approximately 18 miles under water in the Pacific Ocean. Resulting tsunami waves reached heights of 133 feet and traveled as far as 6 miles inland. This same earthquake moved Honshu, the main island of Japan, 8 feet east and shifted the entire planet on its axis an estimated 4 to 10 inches.

The deadly wave that roared up the Tagus River in Lisbon in 1755 was a tsunami. Not all major earthquakes create these enormous waves. An earthquake in the middle of a continent, for example, is unlikely to result in a tsunami.

Earthquakes that take place on the floor of the world's oceans are responsible for tsunamis.

When tectonic plates on the ocean floor suddenly slip and one plate moves underneath another, the sudden motion and release of energy pushes up an enormous amount of ocean water. The water spreads out in every direction from the epicenter of the earthquake, traveling in the deep ocean at speeds up to 500 miles per hour.

Out in the deep ocean, a tsunami causes little damage. But, as the tsunami approaches shallower water near land, its destructive force can grow immense. In what is known as the shoaling effect, the contour of the land causes the wave to slow down and rapidly grow in height.

As the water gets shallower and there is less space for the energy of the wave to spread into, the water coming up behind the front of the wave has nowhere to go but up. Its wave length diminishes and its amplitude (or height) dramatically increases.

Remember—wave amplitude equals wave strength. A tsunami can land with incredible strength, reaching amplitudes that range from several feet to more than 1,000 feet.

Aceh, Indonesia, in the aftermath of the 2004 earthquake and tsunami

EARTHQUAKES AND FIRE

Earthquakes do not cause fires, but out-of-control fires following an earthquake frequently cause more damage and death than the shaking of the ground itself. That was the case with the earthquake that struck San Francisco, California, in 1906.

The 7.9-magnitude earthquake ruptured gas lines and caused the outbreak of more than 30 fires, which destroyed about 90 percent of the city.

A similar tragedy befell Tokyo, Japan, in 1923, when an earthquake struck during the lunch hour. People throughout the city were cooking meals over open flames, which caused widespread fires. When more than 35,000 people sought shelter in an Army clothing depot, they were killed when a fire tornado engulfed the building. In more recent times, the 1995 Great Hanshin earthquake in Kobe, Japan, resulted in nearly 300 fires sweeping over the city.

DISASTER FACT

When an earthquake creates a tsunami, it is nearly always the tsunami that causes more death and destruction than the shaking of the land.

EARTHQUAKE PREPAREDNESS

Earthquakes cannot be prevented, and geologists have not yet developed the technology to predict exactly when an earthquake will strike. The best we can do to prevent damage and death from earthquakes is to take defensive measures.

Buildings can be made both stronger and more flexible to withstand the violent shaking that occurs during a major earthquake. Engineers dedicate time and other resources to test different materials and designs to find combinations that will save the most lives in the event of an earthquake.

Take a look at some footage from different historical earthquakes in this video.

San Francisco Nat Geo earthquake

San Francisco on fire after the 1906 earthquake

credit: Chadwick, H. D.

Tsunami warning signs at Ko Poda Beach, Thailand

Communities can protect themselves by not allowing buildings to be constructed on land that is known to be prone to soil liquefaction.

International, national, and regional tsunami warning systems continue to develop faster, more efficient means of alerting populations to the impending danger. Many coastal communities now have evacuation plans in place and buildings are being constructed to make it easier for people to quickly escape to higher ground.

Earthquakes happen when the power that's contained in the movement of the tectonic plates translates into destruction on the surface of the earth. While hundreds of earthquakes happen every day, only a few are considered to be natural disasters because of the consequences on the human population.

In the next chapter, we'll turn our attention to another natural disaster that gets its energy from the earth—volcanoes!

- **What is the relationship between drifting tectonic plates and earthquakes?**

- **Why were scientists initially reluctant to claim that Earth was once made up of a single landmass?**

- **Does the knowledge that hundreds of earthquakes take place around the world every day change your perception of our planet? Why or why not?**

VOCAB LAB 📖

Write down what you think each word means. What root words can you find to help you? What does the context of the word tell you?

amplitude, **crust**, **earthquake**, **epicenter**, **fault line**, **fissure**, **mantle**, and **tectonic plates**.

Compare your definitions with those of your friends or classmates. Did you all come up with the same meanings? Turn to the text and glossary if you need help.

MAKE A SHAKE TABLE

Engineers use a device called a shake table to test their ideas when designing earthquake-resistant structures. In this activity, you will build your own shake table using common household objects.

- **Place two pieces of sturdy cardboard together, about 8½ inches by 11 inches, and slide two rubber bands around the wide ends of both pieces of cardboard.** Space the rubber bands about 4 inches apart.

- **Slide four tennis balls in between the two pieces of cardboard.** Position them underneath each of the rubber bands.

- **Use masking tape to attach a paint stirrer underneath the top piece of cardboard.**

- **To test your shake table, hold the bottom piece of cardboard with one hand while you pull and release the handle with your other hand.** The top piece of cardboard should shake back and forth as if it were land moving during an earthquake.

To investigate more, construct a model building about 6 inches high to test on your shake table. Use building materials such as marshmallows and toothpicks, modeling clay, popsicle sticks, or anything else you want. Place your building on your shake table and pull the top layer of cardboard to make it shake. What happens? How can you improve your building design?

Chapter 2
Volcanoes: A Burping Earth

Why are volcanoes some of the deadliest natural disasters?

Volcanoes not only cause destruction during and right after an eruption, they can continue to cause suffering long after the actual explosion by altering weather and air conditions around the planet.

On August 27, 1883, people in 50 different parts of the world heard the loudest sound that had ever been recorded on Earth. The sound originated on the uninhabited island of Krakatoa, located in the Sunda Strait in the country of Indonesia on the eastern edge of the Indian Ocean.

The sound waves of this remarkable phenomenon traveled around the globe four times. As those sound waves passed by the island of Rodrigues, 3,000 miles to the west from where the sound originated, people reported hearing something that resembled the roar of heavy gunfire.

Krakatoa was a volcanic island. From May through August 1883, it blew itself apart with a series of deadly eruptions. Two of those explosions created enormous waves of hot ash, gas, and lava fragments that rolled down the sides of the island. They hit the waters of the Sunda Strait with so much force they created tsunamis. The eruptions ejected enough volcanic material into the atmosphere to affect weather patterns around the globe for the next five years.

Anak Krakatoa slowly emerged from the waters of the Sunda Strait after the original Krakatoa blew itself apart in 1883.

It is estimated that the eruptions of Krakatoa, along with their resulting tsunamis, claimed the lives of more than 36,000 people.

THINGS IN COMMON

Earthquakes and volcanoes share a lot in common. Both are awesome natural events that can cause tremendous amounts of harm to human populations, and both are difficult for humans to predict when they will happen. But earthquakes and volcanoes are even closer cousins in terms of the processes that create them—plate tectonics.

Have you ever gazed up at a mountain and wondered where it came from? The answer to that question lies beneath our feet in the earth's crust, where tectonic plates push against one another with enough force to lift huge swaths of Earth's crust upward. This doesn't happen overnight. It takes hundreds, thousands, even millions of years for mountains to form. But, eventually, there they are!

KRAKATOA 2018

In the years following the 1883 eruption of Krakatoa, another volcanic mountain arose in its place. Called Anak Krakatoa, or Child of Krakatoa, the new volcano rose above the waterline in the Sunda Strait in 1930. Growing at a rate of 5.1 inches per week since the 1950s, Anak Krakatoa was active on and off for decades when it finally erupted in full force in late December 2018. As in the past, the eruption was followed by tsunamis, believed to have been caused by undersea landslides. They claimed the lives of hundreds of people on the coastal islands of Java and Sumatra.

This 1888 lithograph depicts the 1883 eruption of Krakatoa.

credit: Parker & Coward, Britain

The Ural Mountains in Russia are
an example of fold mountains.

The Sierra Nevada Mountains in
California are block mountains.

Mount Merapi in Indonesia
is a volcanic mountain.

For example, the Swiss Alps in Switzerland are the product of the long-term collision between the African plate and the Eurasian plate. The Himalaya Mountains, the highest on Earth, are the result of the Indo-Australian plate moving steadily toward the Eurasian plate.

The movement of tectonic plates creates three different types of mountains: fold, block, and volcanic.

- **A fold mountain forms when one plate rides over another and one plate buckles and folds.** They are some of the largest mountain ranges in the world, including the Urals in Russia, the Rocky Mountains in the United States, and the Andes in the Southern Hemisphere.

- **A block mountain arises when fault lines in a plate break apart, forming "blocks" of crust.** One block sinks, another rises, and a mountain is the result.

- **Volcanic mountains come into being by volcanic activity taking place along the boundaries of tectonic plates.** Molten rock erupts from deep inside Earth's core and then cools on the surface. If this happens long enough and often enough, a volcanic mountain, such as Krakatoa, will form.

THE SCIENCE OF NATURAL DISASTERS | CHAPTER TWO

WHERE VOLCANOES FORM

If you look at a map of active volcanoes in the world, you will see that none of them are located in the deep interior of a country. It's because volcanoes form along the boundaries of the tectonic plates. That is, volcanoes form along the edges of continents, where ocean meets land.

As with the majority of earthquakes, most volcanoes are found along the 25,000-mile stretch of the Ring of Fire. Three-fourths of the world's active volcanoes are located in the Ring of Fire. All but three of the world's largest eruptions during the last 11,000 years took place somewhere along the ring.[1]

The active volcanoes that show up on a map represent only a portion of all the volcanic activity taking place on the planet. A tremendous amount of volcanic activity also takes place along the boundaries of tectonic plates on the ocean floors. We don't see them, but they are there—vast volcanic mountain ranges that dwarf the mountains we admire above sea level.

The Mid-Atlantic Ridge, located along the floor of the Atlantic Ocean, forms part of the longest mountain range on the planet.

WHAT IS VOLCANIC ACTIVITY?

Volcanic activity is when magma, lava, ash, and hot gases flow or are ejected through an opening in Earth's crust during an eruption. As with earthquake activity, volcanic activity takes place constantly around the planet but only rarely causes a natural disaster. Most volcanic activity on the planet is of no immediate consequence to people at all.

A map of the Mid-Atlantic Ridge

credit: NOAA

VOLCANIC ERUPTIONS

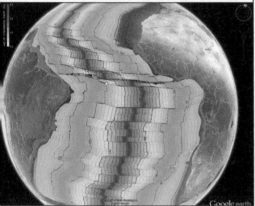

New ocean floor is created as the seismic activity continues and lava erupts under the water along the Mid-Atlantic Ridge. This map shows that new land being pushed away from the fissure as more new land forms.

credit: NOAA Office of Ocean Exploration and Research, 2016 Hohonu Moana

Whether under the ocean or on a landmass, volcanic activity can be peaceful. If a volcano is dormant, meaning not active, people can live at the base of a volcano for centuries with no need for alarm.

Even when a volcano is active, it isn't necessarily dangerous. Puffs of steam rising out of the top of a volcano is no reason for people at the base to run for their lives. It's only when there is a violent volcanic eruption that volcanoes go from being harmless neighbors to natural disasters. The question is: What makes a volcano erupt?

Our world is composed of 92 naturally occurring elements, such as iron and gold. Eight of these make up more than 98 percent of Earth's crust.

- 46.6 percent oxygen (O)
- 27.7 percent silicon (Si)
- 8.1 percent aluminum (Al)
- 5.0 percent iron (Fe)
- 3.6 percent calcium (Ca)
- 2.8 percent sodium (Na)
- 2.6 percent potassium (K)
- 2.1 percent magnesium (Mg)

As you can see, oxygen and silicon form most of Earth's crust. Oxygen and silicon are also the two main components of magma. To understand how and why volcanoes erupt, we need to explore the chemistry of magma.

Oxygen carries a negative atomic charge (-2). Silicon carries a positive atomic charge (+4). Oxygen and silicon atoms are attracted to one another. When they link up, they form a strong chemical bond and they can create chains, sheets, and even vast networks of magma.[2]

Magma is viscous, or thick. Trapped within the highly viscous magma are dissolved gases. These include water vapor, carbon dioxide, sulfur dioxide, hydrogen sulfide, and hydrogen halides. When magma rises to the surface, the pressure decreases and these gases are released from the liquid portion of the magma.

What happens when you open a bottle of carbonated beverage such as soda?

There's a fizzy sensation and sound! And, if the bottle has been shaken, sometimes it can explode all over you! This fizzing and exploding is from pressure being released and the carbon dioxide escaping.

This same process takes place in volcanic activity when magma reaches the surface and pressure is released. The chemical bonds that held the dissolved gases in place are suddenly broken and the result is an explosive burst of energy a little bigger than the one that sometimes happens in your kitchen.

THREE TYPES OF MAGMA

Whenever magma rises up to the surface of Earth's crust, those dissolved gases—mostly water vapor—are released. But eruptions are not always violent events.

Magma is a mixture of minerals and water, and the type of eruption that occurs depends both on the chemical makeup of the magma and whether anything is blocking the release of that magma. Let's look first at three basic types of magma.

What created the loudest sound ever recorded in human history? The eruption of a volcano. Listen to Krakatoa erupting at this website.

🔍 Krakatoa sound

Basaltic magma eruption

Andesitic magma eruption

- **Basaltic magma is the most abundant and least viscous magma.** Formed at high temperatures, it flows easily and any gases trapped inside can escape without causing a big commotion. Basaltic magma produces mild eruptions.

- **Andesitic magma has a higher silicon-oxygen content than basaltic magma and forms at lower temperatures.** Therefore, it is more viscous, which means it flows less easily, than basaltic magma. When pressure is released on the gases trapped inside andesitic magma, they escape with more force. Andesitic magma may produce large, dramatic explosions, with gray clouds roiling the sky far above the top of the volcano.

Rhyolitic magma eruption

- **Rhyolitic magma has the highest silicon-oxygen content, forms at very low temperatures, and is highly viscous.** It produces the most dramatic and violent eruptions, sending hot ash and gas miles high into the atmosphere and releasing rivers of molten lava.

Depending on what kind of magma is rising to the surface of the crust, the volcanic explosions will be small, medium, or large.[3]

WHY DO WE LIVE NEAR VOLCANOES?

Knowing that volcanoes might erupt and cause untold amounts of damage, why have people ever chosen to live near volcanoes in the first place? Civilizations have prospered around volcanoes because, when they are not erupting, they can be great places to live. The soil around volcanoes tends to be rich with nutrients (good for growing crops), the rock formations around volcanoes tend to create good natural harbors (vital for commerce), and many volcanoes arise in valleys that are easy to defend against invaders (good homeland security). Throughout history, the benefits of having a volcano in the backyard have outweighed the risks.

The city of Kagoshima, Japan, is one of many populated areas around the world that have sprung up in the shadows of active volcanoes. More than 600,000 people live within sight of Mount Sakurajima.

PARTS OF A VOLCANO

Most volcanoes are located atop a magma chamber, a large reservoir of liquid rock found deep within the planet. Magma chambers are subject to tremendous amounts of pressure. When that pressure eventually cracks the rock surrounding the magma chamber, the molten rock can then rise to the surface. When it does, a volcanic eruption occurs.

The conduit of a volcano is the tunnel that provides a way for magma to rise up from deep in the earth to the surface. But don't imagine a conduit as a single pipe leading up to the top of a volcano. Most large volcanoes have multiple conduits—a primary conduit with smaller conduits coming off of it like the branches on a tree. Magma can escape both from the top of a volcano and from the sides.

The vent, or throat, of a volcano is the opening where volcanic material is ejected. As with conduits, there can be multiple vents. But there will be only one main vent, connected to the primary conduit.

Explosive eruptions often create large, bowl-shaped cavities, called craters, at the top of volcanoes. Craters form around the central vent. The flanks, or slopes, of a volcano are its sides. Steep flanks are created by explosive eruptions of volcanic material. More gradual flanks are created by slowing flowing magma.

HOW VOLCANOES CAUSE DAMAGE

The damaging effects of a violent volcanic eruption come in two forms—immediate and long-term. The immediate effects are fairly easy to spot. Depending on its viscosity, red hot lava may roll quickly or slowly down the side of a mountain, burning everything in its path.

WHERE MAGMA ESCAPES

Our classic concept of an explosive volcanic eruption always shows the magma and the eruption column of volcanic ash shooting out of the crater, right at the top of the volcano. That is, in fact, the most common area of release, since the crater tends to be the weakest point of the volcano.

But the crater isn't *always* the weakest point. Highly pressurized magma will escape wherever it can, including the flanks of a volcano. In May 1980, Mount St. Helens in Washington State violently erupted on its northern flank. The eruption created the largest landslide ever recorded and sent an eruption column 15 miles into the atmosphere.

Pyroclastic flows, which are the enormous clouds of gas and ash released by a volcano, can be both poisonous and extremely hot.

They can destroy vegetation for miles around and cause human and animal deaths by suffocation. When Mount Vesuvius erupted in August 79 CE in Italy, for example, there was so much gas and ash released and it was so toxic that people died almost immediately.

Explosive volcanic eruptions can also set off earthquakes. The sudden release of magma along the boundaries of tectonic plates can cause the plates to move, resulting in a quake. This happened in late December 2018, when an eruption of Italy's Mount Etna was followed by a 4.8-magnitude earthquake that rocked the island of Sicily two days later.

As we saw with the 1883 eruption of Mount Krakatoa, volcanoes can also produce deadly tsunamis. In the case of Krakatoa, the tsunamis resulted when an enormous pyroclastic flow hit the waters of the Sunda Strait. An earthquake triggered by a volcano can have the same effect.

Pyroclastic flows on Mount Mayon, in the Philippines, in 1984

LONG-TERM EFFECTS

The immediate effects of a violent volcanic eruption can be both horrifying and mesmerizing. The long-term effects are much less spectacular but far more consequential. When an eruption is large enough to send an eruption column dozens of miles into the atmosphere, it can cause damage around the world. It does this by affecting global weather systems, sometimes for years after the initial eruption.

ALONE AMONG NATURAL DISASTERS

Volcanic eruptions are unique among natural disasters. They are the only natural disasters that can have an impact on the entire world. Most volcanic activity causes no harm to humans at all. Some volcanic activity results in destruction to a small, isolated area. But when a volcanic eruption projects ash and gas into the stratosphere, that volcanic material can be carried around the globe and the whole world can be affected.

The atmosphere that surrounds planet Earth is divided into five different spheres, but we are going to discuss just two of them—the troposphere, the layer closest to the surface of Earth, and the next layer above, the stratosphere.

The troposphere extends about 6 to 7 miles from the surface of Earth. This is where all our weather takes place! If the height of an eruption column is restricted to the troposphere, the affects of ash and poisonous gases that were released will be limited to a relatively small area. Soon, rains will wash dangerous particles out of the troposphere.

Long-term global consequences set in, however, when an eruption column propels volcanic material into the stratosphere. Located anywhere from 8 to 30 miles above Earth's surface, the stratosphere is where jet airplanes fly at cruising altitudes. This is also where narrow rivers of air, known as jet streams, carry currents of air around the globe.

Too much water vapor or carbon dioxide let loose in the jet streams after a volcanic eruption can warm the planet for years to come. On the flip side, massive amounts of sulfur dioxide set adrift in the jet streams may block the sun's rays from penetrating Earth's atmosphere. The result can be lower temperatures throughout large parts of the globe. Vast amounts of ash can also block the sun's rays and lower temperatures.

FORECASTING VOLCANIC ERUPTIONS

When it comes to predicting when a volcano will violently erupt, volcanologists—scientists who study volcanoes—are in the same boat as the seismologists who study earthquakes. They can't say for sure when the next natural disaster will strike.

But it's not for lack of trying. Governments and scientific organizations have established volcano observatories around the world, putting many volcanoes under constant monitoring. Some clues to possible eruptions have been detected, such as the frequency and strength of underlying earthquakes or ground deformation caused by changes in magma from the interior of the volcano.

Still, with more than 50 explosive eruptions taking place each year somewhere on the planet, volcanoes continue to take us by surprise.

A DEADLY NATURAL DISASTER

Iceland is one of the most volcanically active places on the planet, and it is in Iceland that many experts believe the deadliest natural disaster in human history took place. In the summer of 1783, there was a series of volcanic eruptions along a 15-mile-long fissure that bisects Mount Laki. Eruptions continued for eight months, leaving 600 square miles of land covered with a 50-foot-thick layer of lava.

THE ASH OF MOUNT TAMBORA

The eruption of Mount Tambora in Indonesia in the spring of 1815 is one of the largest eruptions ever recorded. Jet streams carried ash from Tambora's eruption column around the globe. That summer, 7,000 miles away in London, England, the landscape artist J.M.W. Turner (1775–1851) captured on canvas the suddenly brilliant sunsets that were produced by the unseen ash particles in the atmosphere. Of much greater consequence was the 1816 "Year Without Summer." As ash particles lingered in the stratosphere, temperatures worldwide fell by nearly 1 degree. The resulting massive crop failures resulted in food shortages and widespread famine.

Present-day Mount Tambora

credit: Tisquesusa (CC BY 4.0)

A row of craters along the Laki fissure in Iceland.

credit: Anne Schöpa (CC BY 3.0)

Of far greater consequence, however, was the release of massive amounts of poisonous gases. About 8 million tons of hydrogen fluoride poisoned and killed humans, livestock, freshwater fish, and crops throughout Iceland. Starvation followed.

Worse still was the release of unheard-of quantities of sulfur dioxide. This heavy compound was ejected into the stratosphere and made its way to Europe. It burned the throats of agricultural workers in England and killed them by the tens of thousands, making it impossible for full harvests to be brought in.

Worldwide, temperatures fell dramatically, freezing Europeans to death in the winter and causing low crop yields during the harvest season. From Egypt to Japan, blocked sunlight also resulted in famines that claimed hundreds of thousands of lives. An exact death toll from the Laki eruptions will never be established, but it is estimated in the millions.

Now that we know something about a natural disaster that forms underground, let's take a look at one that forms in the air—hurricanes!

Take a look at footage from the 1973 fissure eruptions in Iceland. Why do you think people rebuilt after this disaster?

 1973 Iceland eruption video

KEY QUESTIONS

- Why are earthquakes and volcanoes found in the same areas around the world? What features do they share in common?

- In what way does magma behave like a bottle of soda? Why is this important for our understanding of what causes a volcanic eruption?

- Why are the long-term effects of a volcanic eruption more damaging than the immediate ones?

Heat in the earth's interior sets the tectonic plates in motion and creates volcanic activity. That's hard to imagine, but in this activity, you're going to demonstrate how heat beneath the earth's surface breaks apart and moves the crust of the earth.

- **Pour a layer of milk that covers the bottom of a saucepan.** Set the saucepan on a hot plate or stovetop burner. Cover the milk with a thick layer of cocoa powder.

- **Turn your heat source to its lowest temperature.** Start a timer running.

- **Make notes on what you observe every two minutes.**

  - How much time passed before you noticed any changes taking place?

  - Where did the first changes take place—around the edges of the earth's crust or at the center? Why did the changes take place there first?

  - How is what you observe in the saucepan similar to processes taking place in the earth's crust?

To investigate more, allow the pan to cool down, then turn the heat source on again. What happens to the earth's crust then?

VOCAB LAB

Write down what you think each word means. What root words can you find to help you? What does the context of the word tell you?

conduit, **crater**, **dormant**, **magma**, **pyroclastic flows**, **stratosphere**, **viscous**, and **volcano**.

Compare your definitions with those of your friends or classmates. Did you all come up with the same meanings? Turn to the text and glossary if you need help.

A MONTH OF MAPPING

Volcanologists keep track of volcanic activity all around the world. They gather information and create databases that can be used for scientific study and to keep at-risk populations informed of any possible dangerous volcanic activity.

Smithsonian volcano report

- **Once a week for four weeks, visit the site of the Smithsonian Institute/USGS Weekly Volcanic Activity Report.** For each volcanic activity that is reported on, collect the following information.

  - Latitude, longitude, and elevation where the activity took place

  - The type of volcano

- **Create a table to record your collected data.** Design a map symbol that you can use to map each volcanic activity on a map of the world.

- **At the end of four weeks, review your data.** What does it reveal about that month of volcanic activity?

  - Where did most of the volcanic activity take place? Was it limited to a certain area or was the activity more widespread?

  - Do you find patterns of volcanic activity at certain latitudes, longitudes, or elevations?

  - Do you see any patterns in the types of volcanoes that were active?

  - Do you see any places where it's possible people might be in danger due to volcanic activity?

To investigate more, visit the website of the World Organization of Volcano Observatories (WOVO) and explore the work being done at a few of the dozens of observatories that are scattered around the globe. What topics are the observatories interested in? How does their geographic location influence what they study?

WOVO observatories

Chapter 3

Hurricanes: Perfect Storms

HURRICANES ARE THE MOST DESTRUCTIVE NATURAL DISASTER, BUT WE CAN'T LIVE WITHOUT THEM.

NEWS FLASH

HURRICANE WANDA HITS THE

What might our planet be like without hurricanes?

Even though hurricanes can cause massive amounts of death and destruction, they are actually critical to the health and well-being of our planet. They are a crucial part of the planet's ability to regulate its temperature to keep it nice and comfortable for humans and other species!

In 1970, the North Indian Ocean produced seven cyclones, but only one of the seven had a direct impact on the course of world history. It was named the Bhola Cyclone, and it roared northeast out of the Indian Ocean into the Bay of Bengal on November 12, 1970. It sank the MV *Mahajagmitra*, a 5,500-ton freighter, killing all 50 people on board, before it made landfall in East Pakistan.

Torrential rains, sustained winds of 165 miles per hour, and a storm surge with a wall of water 20 to 30 feet high wiped out entire villages. It destroyed the fishing industry that fed 75 percent of East Pakistan's population and claimed the lives of an estimated 500,000 people.

Starvation and widespread political unrest quickly followed. Many in East Pakistan blamed the government in Pakistan for bungling relief efforts after the storm. By March 1971, East Pakistan was at war with Pakistan. By December of that same year, East Pakistan was well on its way to becoming the country we now know as Bangladesh.

A natural disaster had created a political one.

How and why do hurricanes form? Why do they only form over water? And why do they sometimes spin in different directions? Let's take a closer look at this awesome force of nature.

DIFFERENT NAMES, SAME THING

The meteorological disaster that ravaged East Pakistan in 1970 goes by many names. Depending on where you live, it might be called a hurricane, a typhoon, a cyclone, a tropical cyclone, or a severe cyclonic storm. Each of those names refers to the same weather event that we will call hurricanes, the standard term used in North America.

But what is a hurricane? At its most basic level, a hurricane is an organized system of rotating clouds and thunderstorms that forms above warm ocean waters. A hurricane never begins its life over the frigid waters of the Arctic Ocean or the dry prairies of the American West or the sweltering deserts of Arabia. Hurricanes always spring into existence above warm ocean waters.

They do so because hurricanes play an essential role in regulating the temperature of our planet. They take enormous amounts of heat from one part of the globe and move it to another. Hurricanes are one of the most destructive of all natural events. However, without them, the world might become uninhabitable.

Image of the Bhola Cyclone taken on November 11, 1970

Planet Earth is exactly the right temperature for life to thrive here. It's the only planet that we know of to claim this trait. But how? And why are the North and South Poles cold? Why is it so hot around the equator? And what keeps the two poles from being even colder or the areas around the equator from being even warmer?

If we can answer those questions, we can understand how hurricanes, despite their destructiveness, help make Earth a hospitable place.

SOLAR RADIATION AND CURRENTS

The sun warms our planet, but it does so unevenly. The sun's rays hit most directly around the equator, turning those parts of the globe into the hottest places on Earth. The sun's rays hit the far northern and southern parts of the planet less directly, leaving them significantly colder.

Global winds moving air around the planet

credit: William Putman/NASA Goddard Space Flight Center

But those places would be even hotter or colder if it were not for the fact that hot air rises and cold air sinks. The movement of hot air rising up from the equator and cold air sinking from around the poles creates global currents in both the atmosphere and the world's oceans.

> Those currents set in motion a kind of global conveyor belt, moving warm water and warm air up to the colder regions and bringing cold water and cold air down to the warmer regions.

This worldwide movement of hot and cold is what keeps the North Pole from getting even colder and oceans and land around the equator from getting even hotter.

WATER, LAND, AND HEAT

The currents alone, however, cannot keep Earth's temperatures in a state of equilibrium between hot and cold. Plus, not all substances on the planet heat up and cool off at the same rate. Land, for example, heats up quickly and cools off quickly. Water, on the other hand, heats up slowly and takes a long time to cool off.

More than 70 percent of our planet is covered by ocean waters. When those tropical and subtropical ocean waters warm up during a long, hot summer, they generate tremendous amounts of heat—much more heat than the oceanic and atmospheric currents can handle.

NAMING HURRICANES

Have you noticed that hurricanes have names, such as Harvey, Irma, Andrew, or Katrina? They are the only natural disasters that get a name, and they get one for a very practical reason. So many hurricanes arise each hurricane season, sometimes at the same time, that meteorologists need a quick and simple way to keep track of them. Currently, the job of naming hurricanes rests with the World Meteorological Organization (WMO).

DISASTER FACT

According to the National Oceanic and Atmospheric Administration (NOAA), 2014 to 2018 were the warmest years ever recorded on Earth. Why? Human activity, from the cars we drive to the way we farm, traps enormous amounts of carbon dioxide in the earth's atmosphere. Carbon dioxide warms the planet.

A water droplet is an example of water in its liquid phase.

An iceberg in the Arctic Ocean is an example of water in its solid phase.

credit: NOAA

Clouds are an example of water in its gas phase.

That's where hurricanes come in. You can almost think of these intense storms as giant engines designed by nature to transport large amounts of heat. They gather up heat off the tropical oceans and carry it north toward the colder regions of the world. Both tropical regions and colder regions benefit from the more even distribution of heat, making each place more comfortable for the living organisms that call those places home.

And it all starts with the most abundant substance on our planet—water.

WATER, WATER EVERYWHERE

Water is one of the most unique substances on Earth and also one of the most ubiquitous. Water is routinely present in our lives in three different forms: solid (ice), liquid (water), and gas (water vapor). Water is ever present. Vast quantities of it cover the planet in all three physical phases.

Water is also crucially important because it has the second-highest heat capacity of any substance on Earth. It is second only to ammonia in its ability to absorb heat.

But it is water, not ammonia, that covers nearly three-fourths of the surface of our planet. The sheer amount of water in the oceans, combined with water's high heat capacity, plays directly into the formation of hurricanes.

FUEL FOR THE HURRICANE

The natural world is ruled by fixed laws. One of these is neatly summed up in the first law of thermodynamics, which states, "Energy is neither created nor destroyed."

What does this have to do with hurricanes?

Imagine a hot summer day, with the sun beating down on the Atlantic Ocean, west of Africa, near the equator. The sun heats the water to the point where individual water molecules can no longer retain the amount of heat, which is a form of energy, that has built up inside of them. Those water molecules evaporate and become water vapor.

Now, here's a question. If energy can neither be created nor destroyed, where has all the energy that warmed up the water gone now that the water is a gas? Has it disappeared? Has it gone somewhere else?

No. That energy is present, stored in the water vapor like electricity in a charged battery. The energy will stay there in a latent form, unused, until some force acts on the water molecules and turns the water vapor back into a liquid. When that happens, the latent energy will be released into the atmosphere and it will warm the air around it.

These processes are called the "latent heat of vaporization" and "the latent heat of condensation." It is the latent heat stored up in countless molecules of water that power the immense force of a hurricane. That's a lot of energy![1]

In 1900, Galveston, Texas, was a thriving city. It had one of the busiest ports in the United States and was widely regarded as the jewel in the crown of Texas. All of that changed on August 17, 1900, when a Category 4 hurricane swept in off the Gulf of Mexico. Hurricane winds tore apart buildings and hurled debris through the air with enough force to kill and a massive storm surge flooded virtually the entire town. By the time the storm passed, an estimated 6,000 people were dead. Property damage was so profound Galveston never regained its position as one of the most important commercial hubs in the United States.

You can see original footage of the aftermath of the Galveston storm at this website. This footage was taken by an assistant of Thomas Edison.

Galveston
original footage

RECIPE FOR A HURRICANE

Not every thundercloud that forms over the oceans turns into a massive storm. Hurricanes are, in fact, finicky things. For a collection of thunderclouds to transform into a hurricane, there are five conditions that must be met.

- The storm clouds must form over warm ocean waters.

- Seawater temperatures must exceed 80 degrees Fahrenheit (27 degrees Celsius) in the upper 200 feet of the ocean.

- The air above the ocean must be warm, humid, and unstable enough to sustain convection. This means the air needs to be moving in a continuous circle of rising hot air and falling cold air.

- Upper-level winds gathering around the storm clouds must be weak and blowing in the same direction that the developing storm is moving in. Strong winds will break the system apart.

- For this entire system of storm clouds to begin rotating, it must be acted upon by the Coriolis effect. This effect is the result of the spinning movement that the planet makes as it rotates on its axis. Different parts of the planet rotate at different speeds because the planet is round. A point just a few feet from either pole is moving at a slower speed than a point on the equator, since the point on the equator has to cover much more distance in the same amount of time. The Coriolis effect deflects circulating air to the right in the Northern Hemisphere and to the left in the Southern Hemisphere.

When all of these conditions are just right, a hurricane might begin to form. But, first, it needs a chimney. Why does a fireplace have a chimney? A chimney creates an updraft that pulls smoke and hot air out of a house and up into the sky. Now, imagine a mass of rotating thunderstorms, with a chimney stuck right in the middle of it. What purpose does that chimney serve? It pulls warm air out of the storm and up into the sky.

Hurricanes, of course, do not have literal, physical chimneys. But they do have something that creates a chimney effect.

As warm moist air rises off the ocean, it actually leaves less air behind. This is called low pressure. That low pressure creates a vacuum, which starts sucking in air to replace the air that was lost.

At the same time that this is happening, the winds of the storm start to spin in an organized fashion around that area of low pressure. This creates a central core that behaves very much like a chimney. It pulls warm air off the ocean and shoots it into the sky. This chimney, or cone, can rise as high as 50,000 feet from the surface of the ocean.

As warm, moist air rises to the top of the cone, water vapor in the air cools and condenses back into water. Latent heat is released, warming the air even more, and creating an even stronger updraft. It pulls up even more warm, moist air from below and hurls it out the top of the cone.

Diagram of a hurricane forming in the Northern Hemisphere

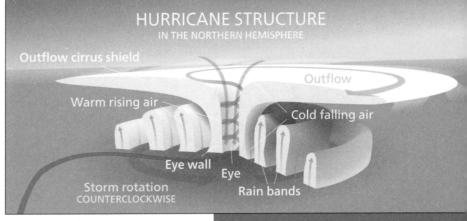

HURRICANE STRUCTURE
IN THE NORTHERN HEMISPHERE

Outflow cirrus shield

Outflow

Warm rising air

Cold falling air

Eye wall

Eye

Storm rotation
COUNTERCLOCKWISE

Rain bands

credit: Kelvinsong (CC BY 3.0)

The more efficiently a central core behaves like a chimney, the stronger a storm will become. If massive amounts of warm air can flow quickly into the core, race up its sides, and exit out the top, a tropical storm will become a hurricane.[2]

A TIME AND A PLACE

Since hurricanes thrive on heat, they are most likely to form during the hot months of summer and fall. The life of a hurricane also depends on weak winds. Springtime over the oceans brings strong winds. By summer, those winds settle down, reaching their lowest speeds in August.

Each of the major oceanic areas has its own hurricane season.

- The Atlantic Ocean season runs from June 1 to November 30.

- The northeast Pacific Ocean season lasts from May to November 30.

- The northwest Pacific Ocean season runs from late June through December.

- The North Indian Ocean season runs from April to December.

Hurricanes are also more likely to form in the Northern Hemisphere. This is due to the fact that there is significantly more water and less land in the Southern Hemisphere. It takes a long time and a lot of energy for the ocean water in the Southern Hemisphere to warm up to 80 degrees, especially when it is cooled by the nearby Antarctic ice sheet. Winds tend to be stronger in the south, too. This prevents hurricanes from forming even if water temperatures are high. It might seem ironic that a storm known for tremendous winds actually depends on there being very weak winds to get its start.

FOUR STAGES OF A HURRICANE

Meteorologists at national hurricane centers watch as storms develop over the oceans. They track the storms and alert the public when a hurricane is headed their way. Before a hurricane is designated a hurricane, however, it must grow through four developmental stages.

- The first stage is a tropical disturbance, marked by a mass of individual thunderstorms with only slight winds.

- The second stage is a tropical depression. It is characterized as a collection of thunderstorms with sustained winds of 23 to 39 miles per hour, with the wind also becoming organized in a circular fashion near the center of the thunderstorms.

- The third stage is a tropical storm. It will show clear signs of a circular shape and have maximum sustained winds of between 39 and 73 miles per hour.

- The fourth stage is a full-blown hurricane, with sustained winds of at least 74 miles per hour and a definite rotation around a central point, called the eye of the storm.

PARTS OF A HURRICANE

We have looked at the central core of a hurricane. Now, let's look at some other parts, starting from the outside and working our way in.

- The outer section is made up of rain bands. These are dense, spiraling clouds that give hurricanes their signature pinwheel appearance. A rain band can be a few miles to 10 miles wide and from 50 to 300 miles long.

NEW ENGLAND HURRICANES

It's relatively rare for hurricanes to make it all the way to New England with the same destructive force as hurricanes that lay waste to more southerly states. But the Great Colonial Hurricane of 1635 and the Great New England Hurricane of 1938 were exceptions. They destroyed wide swaths of Rhode Island, Massachusetts, and Connecticut and hit New Hampshire, Maine, and Vermont with damaging winds and rains. The 1938 storm hit with so much force, it set off seismographs in Alaska. Coastal flooding was so severe, entire villages disappeared into the Atlantic Ocean, never to be seen again.

Flooding in Buzzard's Bay, Massachusetts, after the 1938 hurricane

Watch a documentary about the 1938 New England hurricane, with some dramatic reenactments.

elevisione killer hurricane

Watch what happens when you fly through the eye of a hurricane.

Curious Videos
hurricane eye
wall

- After we pass through the rain bands, we come to the eye wall. This is a ring of thunderstorms, 5 to 30 miles wide. It is the most volatile area of the storm, marked by wind speeds of up to 200 miles per hour and turbulent updrafts and downdrafts.

- Next is the eye, an oasis of serenity. The eye is characterized by low air pressure, calm winds, and clear skies. But it is also remarkably large, reaching a diameter from 20 to 50 miles across.

Look on page 49 to see these parts of a hurricane.

THE PATH OF A HURRICANE

No two hurricanes follow the same path, and the journey that any one hurricane takes can be wildly erratic. In general, however, before a hurricane nears land, its path is largely determined by global wind patterns. Once it nears land, local weather patterns will influence which direction it follows.

This map shows the tracks of all tropical cyclones that formed worldwide from 1985 to 2005.

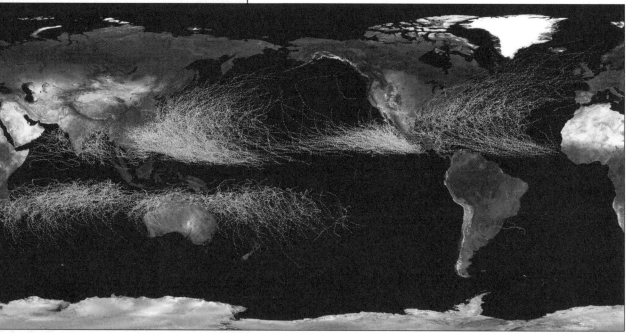

credit: NASA

A hurricane that forms in the Atlantic Ocean off the coast of Africa, for example, will be pushed west across the ocean by winds that blow from east to west. As the storm nears the Caribbean islands and North America, its path will be determined by whatever weather systems it runs into close to land.

If the hurricane encounters a high-pressure zone to its east, it tends to skirt the western edge of that high-pressure zone and spin north. It will head out into the colder waters of the North Atlantic Ocean and disintegrate.

But if the hurricane runs into a high-pressure zone to its west, and if that zone extends far enough to the south, the hurricane will be blocked from taking a northerly course. Instead, it will continue heading west, toward land, including highly populated areas such as Puerto Rico, Mexico, Cuba, and the southern coast of the United States.

WHEN THE STORM HITS

When hurricanes strike, there are three ways that they turn a natural event into a natural disaster. They cause harm with wind, rain, and storm surge.

If you have ever heard news reports about hurricanes, you've no doubt heard them described with an assigned category number. When Hurricane Michael reached the Florida Panhandle on October 9, 2018, for example, it was reported as a Category 4 hurricane.

That number is derived from a scale that rates hurricanes based on sustained wind speeds and the amount of damage to property and trees the winds are expected to cause. It's called the Saffir-Simpson Hurricane Wind Scale. It has five categories, starting at Category 1, with hurricane winds of at least 74 miles per hour, and ending at Category 5, with sustained wind speeds of 157 miles per hour or higher.

Wind damage to homes in Punta Gorda, Florida, after Hurricane Charley, in August 2004

THE RAINS CAME

If wind speeds slow down, will a hurricane cause less damage? That's certainly possible, but there's a catch. The slower a hurricane moves, the more likely it is to leave enormous amounts of rain in its wake.

Exactly how much rain a hurricane produces depends on a variety of factors, but a slow-moving hurricane—or even a tropical storm—can drop trillions of gallons of water on an area in just a matter of hours or days. The resulting floods can cause millions of dollars in property damage and sweep people to their deaths.

The worst-case scenario is a slow-moving hurricane that remains close to a source of water vapor— that water vapor is fuel for the storm. This is what happened when Hurricane Harvey started on its journey from the Caribbean Sea to eastern Texas on August 17, 2017. During Harvey's two-week lifespan, the storm system swung between a hurricane and a tropical storm.

Map plotting the track and intensity of Hurricane Harvey

It stalled over the coastline of eastern Texas and the warm waters of the Gulf of Mexico. In an average September, that region of Texas receives 3 to 4 inches of rain. During the course of just four days, 40 to 60 inches of rain fell!

RISING TIDES

The strong winds and torrential rains of a major hurricane can cause untold amounts of damage. If a storm surge gets added into that already dangerous mix, the cost in human life and destruction of property climbs even higher.

The mechanics of a storm surge are similar to those of a tsunami. A storm surge begins as a large wave that causes no trouble while it remains in deep waters. But it grows to dangerous heights and overwhelms people and property as it approaches shallower grounds.

Flooding in Port Arthur, Texas, in the aftermath of Hurricane Harvey in September 2017.

Remember the shoaling effect of a tsunami? This is the same in the storm surge of a hurricane. The difference is what starts the wave moving in the first place. With a tsunami, the wave is initiated by an earthquake or a volcanic eruption. With a storm surge, the wave forms because of strong winds circulating around the eye of the hurricane over deep ocean waters.

Just like with a tsunami, the water of the storm surge wave piles up on itself as it nears the shore of a coastal area. A storm surge can be dozens of feet high. It can hit with enormous force. The resulting flooding can claim hundreds of lives.

The storm surge created when Tropical Cyclone Mahina struck Bathurst Bay, Australia, on March 5, 1899, was one of the largest ever recorded—a staggering 43 to 48 feet high! Mahina was responsible for more than 300 deaths and remains the deadliest storm in Australia's history.[3]

Bubbles and hurricanes? What's the connection? Read this article to find out what some scientists are trying in an attempt to halt hurricanes.

 bubbles stop hurricanes

KEY QUESTIONS

- **Why might some parts of the planet become uninhabitable without hurricanes?**

- **How does a hurricane derive its energy from water vapor?**

- **Why does a slow-moving hurricane sometimes cause more damage than a fast-moving hurricane with extremely high winds?**

HOW TO STOP A HURRICANE

Scientists have explored various ways to prevent tropical storms from developing into hurricanes. Most ideas focus on how to cool the warm ocean waters that provide hurricanes with their fuel. Researchers have tried to haul icebergs into the Gulf of Mexico, to drop dry ice near developing hurricanes, and to install systems of pipes that can be turned on to create water bubbles coming up from the colder depths of the ocean.

So far, none of these methods has proved effective. For now, the safest thing to do when a hurricane approaches is to get out of its way. You can protect your house by boarding up the windows. You can store your automobiles in garages.

But when major hurricanes are forecast, local government agencies may issue mandatory evacuation orders. This means you must leave the area before the storm strikes.

Such warnings are to be taken seriously. Those who stay behind risk drowning, being stranded in high waters, or watching helplessly as ferocious winds rip the roofs off their houses.

On the plus side—nothing lasts forever! Even the strongest storms eventually run out of energy and fall apart. A hurricane passing over land loses the strength it derives from warm ocean waters, as does a hurricane traveling over colder ocean waters or running into strong winds. No matter how forceful a hurricane is, its lifespan is limited.

AIR PRESSURE EXPERIMENTS

Where meteorological natural disasters are concerned, air pressure is often of critical importance. Yet the fact that air has actual weight and that it pushes against objects is difficult to imagine. These simple experiments can show you air pressure in action!

Experiment No. 1

- **Fill a small cup one-quarter full of water.** Place an index card across the entire opening and carry the cup and index card to a sink. Hold the index card in place, turn the cup and card upside down, and let go of the index card.

- **What happens?** Why? What role does air pressure play in this experiment?

Experiment No. 2

- **Place a ping-pong ball into the wide end of a funnel.** Tip your head back, bring the narrow end of the funnel to your mouth, and blow into it as hard as you can.

- **What happens?** What action is air pressure having on the ping-pong ball?

To investigate more, watch this YouTube video about air pressure and water. What can a balloon, water, and a plastic bottle teach us about the natural world?

air pressure fun science demos

VOCAB LAB

Write down what you think each word means. What root words can you find to help you? What does the context of the word tell you?

Coriolis effect, current, cyclone, equilibrium, hurricane, storm surge, and **water vapor**.

Compare your definitions with those of your friends or classmates. Did you all come up with the same meanings? Turn to the text and glossary if you need help.

CATCH THE WIND

Meteorologists use high-tech anemometers to measure wind speed—a key element of all hurricanes. In its simplest form, however, an anemometer is nothing more than cups that rotate on a center shaft and catch the wind. Each full rotation that the cups make is the equivalent of one mile per hour of wind speed.

* **Study this photograph of an anemometer.** What do you need to do to make your own?

Robinson anemometer

  * base
  * center shaft
  * four rotating arms
  * four cups

* **You might try paper or plastic cups, wooden dowels or plastic drinking straws, soda bottles or modeling clay to make an anemometer.** Experiment with different materials and models until you create a working anemometer. If you get stuck, you might look up DIY anemometers on the internet.

* **To measure wind speed, mark one of the cups of the anemometer with a large dot of color.** Create a breeze in front of your anemometer, using a fan or other device. Set a timer for 30 seconds. As the anemometer turns in the breeze, count the number of rotations. Each full rotation is the equivalent of one mile per hour.

  * How much wind speed are you able to generate using everyday devices?

  * What kind of wind speeds do you measure when you take the anemometer outside?

  * A hurricane has to have sustained winds of at least 74 miles per hour. How much stronger would your breezes have to be before they reached hurricane levels?

To investigate more, explore some of the real-world instruments that meteorologists use to measure the properties of hurricanes and the atmosphere. How do they measure air pressure? How do they measure wind speeds that are faster than moving automobiles?

Chapter 4

Tornadoes: The Sound and the Fury

TORNADOES ARE ONE OF THE MOST DESTRUCTIVE FORCES ON EARTH.

Why do tornadoes feature so often in books and movies?

Scientists don't know much about how tornados form, which can make them seem even more frightening. These incredibly destructive storms cause chaos and destruction with unbelievable strength, making them a very scary possibility in large regions of the United States.

Have you ever watched a science fiction movie where a colossal creature rampages through a city, destroying everything in its path? On April 27, 2011, people in the southeast United States experienced that Hollywood scenario in real life. Only their tormentor was not a sci-fi monster, but a series of tornadoes that ripped through eight states.

Mississippi and Alabama were the hardest hit.

In a single 24-hour period, 216 tornadoes touched down in just those two states. In Philadelphia, Mississippi, a tornado peeled pavement right off the roads and scoured a 2-foot-deep trench through the ground. In Smithville, Mississippi, tornadoes turned solid brick homes into rubble and hurled an SUV into the top of a water tower. In Tuscaloosa and Birmingham, Alabama, tornadoes stripped the bark off of trees, injured 1,500 people, and killed 65 more.

The remains of a brick house in Tuscaloosa, Alabama, April 27, 2011

And that was just one day. In all, this historic outbreak of severe weather lasted three days, from April 25 to April 28. It produced winds up to 210 miles per hour, created hail the size of baseballs, took the lives of 324 people, and caused billions of dollars in property damage. To date, it remains the costliest tornado outbreak on record worldwide.

WHERE THE TORNADOES LIVE

Like all the natural disasters we have examined so far, tornadoes are one of the most violent and destructive forces on Earth. Unlike most other natural disasters, however, tornadoes are unique in where they take place. The vast majority of tornadoes, 70 percent of them, occur in just one spot on the globe—the Great Plains of the North American continent.

DEADLIEST TORNADO OUTBREAK

The 2011 tornado outbreak in the southeast United States was the costliest ever, but it was not the deadliest. That unhappy distinction belongs to the Tri-State Tornado of March 18, 1925. It cut a path of destruction 235 miles long through Missouri, Illinois, and Indiana. In a little more than three hours, it killed 695 people and injured another 2,027.

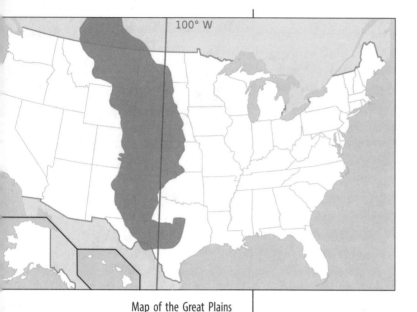

Map of the Great Plains

This is a south-north belt of relatively flat grasslands that includes Kansas, Nebraska, North and South Dakota, Colorado, Iowa, Minnesota, Montana, New Mexico, Oklahoma, Texas, and Wyoming, and the southern portions of the provinces of Alberta, Manitoba, and Saskatchewan in Canada.

Tornadoes also wander into more easterly states, such as Mississippi and Alabama.

HOW TORNADOES FORM

Tornadoes come from thunderstorms, the same kind you see on any dark and stormy day or night when gray clouds gather overhead, thunder and lightning fill the sky, and heavy rains fall.

Luckily, fewer than 10 percent of thunderstorms become tornadoes. Meteorologists remain perplexed as to exactly what triggers a thunderstorm to turn into a twister, but here's what they do know.

An ordinary thunderstorm is made up of two columns of air—an updraft and a downdraft. In one column, warm, moist air rises until it reaches a point in the atmosphere where the air begins to cool. The water vapor condenses, forming clouds that spread out like an icy cap across the sky. The water vapor turns into cold water droplets, which create precipitation—rain or hail—that sinks to the ground. The precipitation produces a downdraft, which pulls in even more cool air from the cloud mass.

Take a look as a tornado forms in this video.

🔍 NatGeo birth tornado

This process forms the second column of air, creating what meteorologists call a single cell thunderstorm. Warm, moist air rises in one column (the updraft) and turns into cool precipitation, which rapidly sinks back to Earth in the second column (the downdraft).

> The mechanics of a single cell thunderstorm are the same as for a super cell thunderstorm, the kind that can become a tornado.

The only major difference is that a super cell has a deep, rotating updraft.

Scientists still don't know why the funnel of a tornado forms. But when it does, rain and hail will fall from the leading side of the storm mass, and the rotating column of air will develop on the trailing side of the storm. And there you have a tornado.

Super cell thunderstorm in New Mexico

THE OTHER 30 PERCENT

If 70 percent of tornadoes occur in North America, where do the other 30 percent occur? They crop up in many places, including South Africa, Europe, Australia, New Zealand, Bangladesh, India, and South America. Tornadoes in these other parts of the world can be just as destructive as those that strike in North America. In June 1967, for example, six tornadoes touched down in the European countries of France, Belgium, and the Netherlands, resulting in 15 deaths and an additional 232 injuries. The big difference between tornadoes in other parts of the world and those in North America is one of frequency. The United States alone experiences 1,200 tornadoes on average each year. Most other areas will experience a few tornadoes a year, if that.

TORNADO SEASON

Like hurricanes, tornadoes have their season each year—typically from March through June. Huge thunderstorms develop during these months as a result of three weather-related events.

- Masses of tropical air flow north from the Gulf of Mexico.

- Cold, dry air flows south from Canada or flows east over the Rocky Mountains at speeds of 50 miles per hour or faster.

- Jet streams moving in an easterly direction collide with the resulting thunderstorm at rates of 150 miles per hour.

If these conditions are just right, these unstable, colliding masses of air will set a thunderstorm into a rotating column that could become a tornado.

credit: Ks0stm (CC BY 4.0)

SHAPE SHIFTING

The classic image of a tornado is one where a spinning funnel of dark clouds stretches down out of the sky to make contact with the ground, where it begins its destructive journey across land. Have you seen the movie *The Wizard of Oz*? Those images are very threatening!

In fact, tornadoes come in a variety of shapes and sizes. A tornado can assume a "wedge" shape, for example, straight-sided and wider than it is tall. Most tornadoes are gray in appearance, but depending on how sunlight hits the clouds, they can also be white.

Even a classic funnel-shaped tornado changes shape during the course of its limited lifespan. In the final moments before they disintegrate, funnel tornadoes frequently thin out and elongate into skinny rope tornadoes.

You might think a stringy tornado causes less damage than the bigger, wider, funnel tornado, but that's not always the case. A rope tornado may actually spin faster than a funnel twister, and it can pack a powerful punch. A rope tornado can rip a house off its foundation the same as a funnel.

PROPERTIES OF A TORNADO

It's nearly impossible to say that an "average tornado" exists. They are, by their very nature, unique meteorological events. They can form in mere minutes and hopscotch across the ground in an utterly haphazard manner. A tornado may flatten an entire neighborhood, but it's equally likely to tear the roof off one house and leave the one right next to it undisturbed.

SPINNING OFFICE CHAIRS

If you have access to a spinning office chair, you can experience the conservation of angular momentum firsthand. Sit in the chair with your arms and legs extended and start spinning the chair. Once you're spinning, pull your arms and legs into the center of the chair. Did you speed up? Now, extend your arms and legs again. Did you slow down? The conservation of angular momentum is a two-way street. It will speed you up as well as slow you down.

Take a look at the radar image tracking of a 2013 tornado in Moore, Oklahoma.

 radar timeline of the Newcastle-Moore EF-5

However, all tornadoes do share some general characteristics.

- The width of a tornado can be as narrow as 7 feet and as wide as 5 miles. On average, however, a tornado is 500 feet across.
- Traveling across land, a tornado can go from being nearly still to accelerating up to 70 miles per hour in a matter of seconds. On average, a tornado moves at about 30 miles per hour.
- Tornadoes have been known to stay on the ground for several hours. On average, a tornado lasts for about 10 minutes.
- The wind speeds of a tornado can range from 40 to 300 miles per hour. And the average? Meteorologists tend not to describe tornadoes in terms of average wind speeds. Instead, they use wind speeds to determine the intensity of a tornado.[2]

BLOWING IN THE WIND

The Fujita Scale, or F-Scale, was created in 1971 by two people—Tetsuya Fujita (1920–1998), a professor at the University of Chicago, where he was known as "Mr. Tornado," and Allen Pearson (1925–2016), a former head of the National Severe Storms Forecast Center. Together, they developed a scale for rating the intensity of tornadoes based on the damage they cause to manmade structures and vegetation.

The scale goes from F0 to F5, starting at "light damage," with winds of 65 to 85 miles per hour, all the way up to "incredible damage," with winds greater than 200 miles per hour. Some meteorologists even include an F6 level—inconceivable damage!

Since Fujita and Pearson first introduced the Fujita Scale, meteorologists have made significant improvements in the way they perform tornado damage examinations. They improved methods to make the scale less open to personal interpretation and to include more types of structures and vegetation. As a consequence, the F Scale is sometimes now referred to as the EF Scale, or Enhanced Fujita Scale.

EFFECTS OF A TORNADO

The aftermath of a tornado can leave an area looking as though it has been struck by a bomb. In fact, the destructive capacity of an EF3 to EF5 tornado is equal to that of an atomic bomb.

The damage a tornado causes to property can be devastating. The winds of a tornado can reduce wood frame and even brick homes to piles of rubble in seconds.

> When a tornado touches down, its funnel behaves as if it were a kind of monstrous vacuum cleaner.

The vortex of rotating air sucks things up into its core and hurls them back out with almost unfathomable force. Houses can be ripped off their foundations and tossed around like playthings. Trees, telephone poles, automobiles, major appliances, boulders, you name it, often meet the same fate.

A tornado on the ground frequently follows a haphazard path. In the bigger picture, though, tornadoes follow highly regular paths as they travel from one part of the country to the next. If you're tracking the path of a tornado across the prairies of North America, you can expect it to travel in a northeasterly direction.

That was precisely the trajectory that a series of rare winter tornadoes took as they made their way through Mississippi and Georgia in late January 2017. A map of the destruction left behind in the wake of one tornado traces a nearly perfect northeast path through Georgia, from Albany to Ashburn to Rochelle.

Damage from a minor tornado in Polk County, Arkansas, in 2008

A scene in Elon, Virginia, after an EF3 tornado struck the town in April 2018

WHAT IS A WEATHER BALLOON?

A weather balloon is just a balloon, usually made out of latex and filled with either helium or hydrogen so that it will rise into the atmosphere. Unlike other balloons, however, a weather balloon is launched with an instrument called a radiosonde attached to it. The radiosonde sends data to meteorologists about atmospheric pressure, temperature, humidity, and wind speed. Weather balloons are routinely launched twice daily at 12-hour intervals at about 800 facilities around the world. When bad weather is brewing, meteorologists will send up additional balloons to help them track the storm.

During a tornado, flying debris is usually the cause of death instead of sheer wind speed. It's easy to understand how a piece of sheet metal ripped off the side of a house and hurled through the air at 300 miles per hour could result in the death of a human being. But in the throes of a major tornado, even otherwise harmless items can become dangerous weapons, too. There have been documented instances, for example, of a tornado throwing a piece of cardboard with enough force for it to lodge in a block of concrete.

STORMY WEATHER

Tornadoes form in a matter of seconds, so it is impossible for meteorologists to predict and warn the public about when a tornado will strike. All tornadoes are born from thunderclouds, however, and meteorologists can predict the arrival of thunderstorms several days in advance.

THE SCIENCE OF NATURAL DISASTERS | CHAPTER FOUR

Using a variety of instruments, such as satellites, weather balloons, and radar, meteorologists keep track of thunderstorms as they develop and stay alert to the possibility that a tornado may be in the making.

A key instrument in the detection of tornadoes is Doppler radar. Conventional radar, which bounces high-frequency radio waves off a developing storm, provides information about only the location and intensity of precipitation. Doppler radar, which bounces microwave signals off of a developing storm, allows meteorologists to see air motion within the storm.

A hook echo on a Doppler radar screen is a good indication that a thunderstorm may become a tornado.

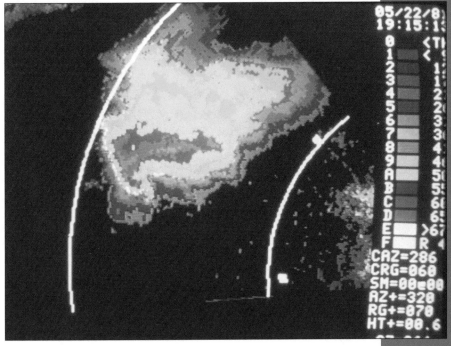

A storm cellar from the 1930s

Using Doppler radar, meteorologists have learned to spot the telltale sign that a tornado is taking shape. When they see a distinct hook at the lower edge of the Doppler radar screen, they know that a tornado may be on the way.

When that hook appears, they send out warnings to emergency broadcast systems.

This doesn't give people much time—maybe 13 to 20 minutes—to prepare for the devastation that may be headed their way. But it's enough time for people to seek shelter, and the heads-up definitely saves lives.

SHELTER FROM THE STORM

What should you do if a tornado is headed your way? Seek shelter—more specifically, find a place where you are protected from flying debris, which is the cause of most tornado-related deaths.

Christie England survived an EF5 tornado in Moore, Oklahoma, in May 2013, by seeking the protection of a storm shelter.

Such places include basements or interior rooms without windows. If you don't have access to a basement, head for a closet, an interior hallway, or a bathroom.

Hiding under a solid piece of furniture, such as a heavy table, offers added protection, as does covering your body with a blanket, sleeping bag, or mattress. Protect your head with whatever you can—bike helmets, motorcycle helmets, even an aluminum bowl! Don't worry what you look like, just be as safe as possible.

In places where hurricanes are prevalent, many homes and businesses include storm shelters specifically designed to protect people from the worst effects of a tornado. If an EF5 tornado is raging all around you, underground is the absolute safest place to be.

Now that you've learned how destructive the moving tectonic plates can be, as well as storms that involve circulating warm and cold air masses, let's see why floods impact so many lives around the world.

KEY QUESTIONS

- **Why don't all thunderstorms turn into tornadoes? What has to happen for a thunderstorm to turn into a tornado?**

- **What aspect of a tornado is most likely to cause serious injury? Where is the safest place to be during a tornado?**

- **Which areas of the planet are least likely to experience a tornado? Can you explain why?**

THE ELECTROMAGNETIC SPECTRUM

Both radio waves and microwaves are electromagnetic waves that exist along the electromagnetic spectrum. There are seven types of waves included in the electromagnetic spectrum. They differ from one another in terms of wave length and wavelength frequency—that is, the distance between one crest of a wave to the next and how frequently the waves are generated. The more frequently a wave occurs, the shorter its wavelength will be. From longest wavelength to shortest, the seven electromagnetic waves are: radio, microwave, infrared, visible, ultraviolet, X-ray, and gamma. Doppler radar uses microwaves.

UNSOLVED MYSTERIES

Scientists still have much to unravel about the mysterious nature of tornadoes, especially how they form in the first place. Investigate the current state of tornado research and create a written and/or visual presentation of what you discover. Use the following questions to help guide your research.

- **Where in the United States does tornado research take place?** Is research being done at universities, government agencies, or a combination of both?

- **What scientific backgrounds are represented in tornado research?** Are all the scientists meteorologists or do they come from other scientific fields as well?

- **What specific things about tornadoes are scientists trying to understand better?** Can you list two or three different things?

- **What kind of tornado research takes place in the field?** What kind of research takes place in laboratories?

- **What is a tornado simulator?** How does it assist in the study of tornadoes? What other types of equipment do the scientists use?

> **To investigate more,** explore what it takes to become a research scientist who studies tornadoes. How much education would you need? What kinds of subjects would you study? Where might you go to school? Where might you find work after your education is completed? Do you think your work as a research scientist would be a rewarding experience? Why or why not?

Chapter 5

Floods: Rivers Rising

How do floods cause so much damage and destruction?

The power of water is immense, and when a lot of water comes together in a short time, the results can be brutal for the structures and living creatures in its path.

At 3,915 miles, the Yangtze River in the People's Republic of China is the third-longest river in the world. It originates in the Tanggula Mountain, more than 16,000 feet above sea level. The Yangtze runs south for hundreds of miles, then makes a 180-degree turn and starts running in a northeasterly direction until it empties into the East China Sea.

Along its journey, the Yangtze takes in the water of 49 tributaries and passes through dozens of major cities. It plays an integral role in the culture and economy of the Chinese people.

In 1931, the great Yangtze River flooded, creating one of the worst natural disasters of the twentieth century. What led to the flooding? Two years of drought, followed by an extraordinarily harsh winter, which deposited abnormally large amounts of snow and ice in the mountains. When the spring thaw started, it coincided with unusually heavy rains. Flooding set in.

By June, people along the lower reaches of the river were abandoning their homes. At least 150,000 people had drowned. Things went from bad to worse when the country was hit with a series of nine cyclones, adding tremendous amounts of water to an area already oversaturated with precipitation. In August, a high-water mark on the Yangtze River in the city of Wuhan was recorded at 53 feet above average.

Other rivers flooded as well, eventually inundating an area the size of New York, New Jersey, and Connecticut combined. Accurate death tolls have been impossible to confirm. Historians currently estimate that the 1931 floods affected 53 million people, killing between 3 and 4 million. Many died of starvation, as the floods destroyed enormous stretches of farmland. But the vast majority of deaths resulted from diseases, which ravaged millions of displaced peoples struggling to survive in crowded, unsanitary conditions.

The Yangtze River in the People's Republic of China

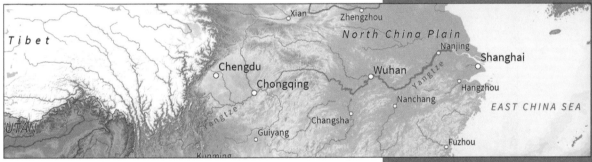

credit: Tan Wei Liang Byorn (CC BY 3.0)

We have seen how earthquakes, volcanoes, and hurricanes can cause catastrophic flooding through tsunamis and storm surges. But there are other types of floods that qualify as natural disasters, too. These floods occur when the surface ground's capacity to absorb precipitation is overwhelmed. It causes rivers and streams to overflow their banks or dry riverbeds to suddenly become raging waterways.

Under the right conditions, these types of floods can occur anywhere in the world. They are not limited to low-lying coastal areas or lands adjacent to major rivers. It's far less common for floods to occur in the tropics, the plains, or the deserts, but they do happen.

Anywhere that an accumulation of water is greater than what the ground surface can absorb, the potential for flood exists. Let's take a closer look at the channels where it happens—the rivers.

WHAT'S A RIVER FOR?

Throughout human history, rivers have played a major role in the rise of civilizations. Great civilizations grow up along the banks of great rivers. The Nile in Africa, the Mississippi in the United States, the Volga in Russia, the Ganges in India, the Yangtze in China—each of these waterways offers a wealth of resources. They give us water for drinking and irrigation, a "road" leading from one settlement to the next, a means to transport goods, a food source, and much more.

Rivers are incredibly important to humanity's survival and cultural development. Explore some of the most important rivers in the world in this web article.

Touropia rivers world

The Nile River as it flows through the city of Cairo, Egypt

credit: U.S. Air Force photo/Senior Airman Sara Csurilla

Rivers are so vital to humanity, it's easy to forget that their role in the natural order has nothing to do with us. Why do rivers exist? They exist so that when precipitation, in the form of rain, snow, sleet, or hail, can't be absorbed into the ground, it will find its way to the oceans. Rivers are simply channels for water to drain to the sea.

If you follow a river from its beginning to its end, you will occasionally discover it emptying into an enclosed lake—but that's rare. The majority of rivers, large and small, carry water out into the open oceans. One river may connect with numerous tributaries before it reaches its destination, but all that water is headed for the ocean.

> Rivers carry water, but they carry something else as well—sediment.

As the water in a river moves along, it picks up a variety of solid materials, including rocks, minerals, and the remains of plants and animals. In a process known as erosion, the river picks up sediment from one place and deposits it in another.

How much sediment a river picks up and how far it carries the sediment load depends on a number of factors, such as how quickly the water is moving and how steep a gradient the water is traveling down. But the sediment amounts can be enormous. The Mississippi River, for example, carries an estimated 500 million tons of sediment into the Gulf of Mexico every year.[1]

THE WATER CYCLE

Water on Earth is always in motion and always changing, from liquid to solid to gas. The water cycle, also called the hydrologic cycle, describes that movement. It starts with water evaporating, primarily off the oceans, and turning into water vapor, a gas. The water vapor condenses into liquid precipitation in the form of rain, snow, hail, or sleet. That precipitation falls to Earth and collects in a number of places. Some of it is absorbed into the ground. Some is frozen into glaciers. The rest collects in ponds, lakes, streams, and rivers, where it is carried back out to the oceans, and the cycle begins again.

Diagram of the water cycle

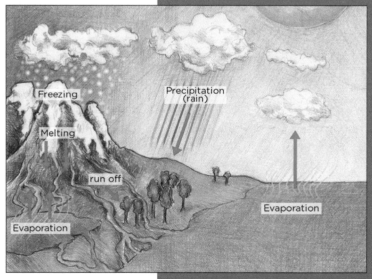

credit: Siyavula Education (CC BY 2.0)

The Mississippi River as it flows through the city of New Orleans, Louisiana. The water is brown due to the sediment load the river is carrying out to the Gulf of Mexico.

As a natural process, river erosion historically has been hugely beneficial to our planet. For centuries, the annual flooding of the Nile River, for example, has deposited tons of nutrient-rich soil, which forms vital farmlands.

Today, scientists are also discovering a new benefit of river erosion. The sediment deposited in wetland areas is rich in stored carbon.

This keeps carbon out of the atmosphere and reduces global warming.[2]

HOW RIVERS BEHAVE

Why do rivers overflow their banks? That seems like a simple question. Rivers overflow their banks when there is more water than the river channel can hold.

However, they try very hard not to overflow their banks. All rivers, regardless of size or location, naturally seek a state of dynamic equilibrium. They constantly respond to change in ways that keep their channels functioning in the most efficient manner possible, so that water and sediment flow to an ocean.

If you have ever seen a river swollen with the spring runoff of snow melting from the mountains, you probably can picture how a river first responds to a sudden influx of water. The river flows more energetically and rapidly. That's a process you can see with your own eyes. What's less obvious, however, are the other ways the river is responding so as to slow down the flow of water and return to its natural equilibrium.

- The rapidly flowing water is eroding the bottom of the riverbed—this will make the gradient less steep and slow down the water.

- That uptick in erosion creates additional sediment—this adds material to the flow of water and increases its viscosity, which also slows it down.

- The river will become more sinuous, forming curves known as meanders—this will lengthen the river channel, which slows the water.

- The motion of excess water also causes the river channel to widen from side to side—this enables the river to accommodate more water and to slow down.

FEEDBACK LOOPS

The dynamic equilibrium at work in a river is an example of a negative feedback loop. In a negative feedback loop, any change in the system provokes a response that seeks to return the system to its original state. All streams and rivers operate on this principle. They react to change by attempting to return to the way they were before that change occurred. A negative feedback loop sounds, well, negative, but in fact, it makes for a very stable environment. A positive feedback loop makes for a less stable environment. In a positive feedback loop, a change in the system provokes a response that seeks to amplify the change. How would a river behave if it operated according to a positive feedback loop? Can you imagine what some of the consequences would be?

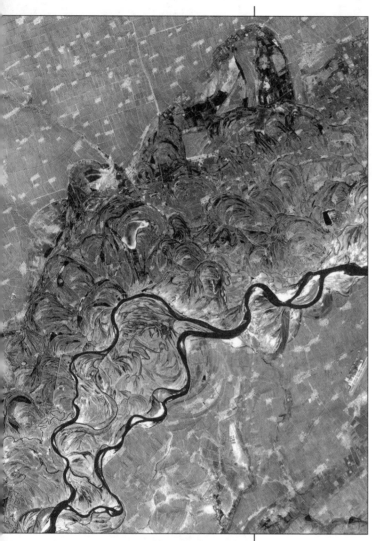
You can see the meanders in the Songhua River in China.

TOO MUCH SEDIMENT

When you see the water in a river channel flowing rapidly, you might assume the flow is forceful due to an increase in the amount of water. That can certainly be the case. But a river can also increase the force of its flow in order to accommodate an excess of sediment.

How can a river make water flow faster without more water being added into the stream?

It accomplishes this trick by using the excess sediment itself, depositing it on the riverbed in such a way that the gradient becomes steeper.

The dynamics are the same as a ramp on a toy race car set. The steeper the ramp, the faster the car will go. So it is with a river. If it requires more force to move sediment through the stream—and there is no increase in water to get the job done—the river creates a sediment ramp that makes water flow faster, with more force, to carry the excess sediment away.

A river dealing with excess sediment might also start to straighten out. Water moves faster and more forcefully through a straight channel than it does through a series of meanders. As time goes by, the banks of the river may erode so as to make the river channel less sinuous.

TYPES OF FLOODS

When the surface ground can no longer absorb more precipitation and a river has lost the battle to maintain its equilibrium, the conditions are set for flooding. The excess water has to go somewhere. Not all floods, however, result in a natural disaster.

A thunderstorm that occurs over a rural meadow, for example, may cause a stream to overflow its banks without causing any harm to a human population.

That same thunderstorm over a highly urban area, however, may cause considerable damage. It takes a relatively small amount of precipitation for paved streets lined with buildings to suddenly flood with 1 or more feet of rushing water.

Regardless of where a flood occurs, it will take one of two major forms—a flash flood or a regional flood.

IN A FLASH

Flash floods are aptly named hydrologic events. They arrive without warning and sometimes depart just as quickly as they came—in a flash! As short-lived as they are, however, they can be devastating natural disasters. In the United States, for example, flash floods cause the majority of all flood-related deaths.

THE POWER OF MOVING WATER

If you come upon moving water in a street, do not walk or drive an automobile through it! Just 1 foot of moving water exerts 500 pounds of force. Two feet of moving water exerts 1,000 pounds of force. But at that 2-foot level, moving water also creates a buoyant uplift of 1,500 pounds. That's more than enough force and uplift to pick up automobiles and carry them away. A startling 50 percent of all flood-related deaths in the United States are related to automobiles.

Flash flooding in New York State

You can see flash flooding and hear about some of the causes in this video.

science 360
flash flood

All it takes to create a flash flood is a thunderstorm. In as little as three or four hours, a single thunderstorm can produce the equivalent of a year's worth of rain. That's a lot of precipitation in a short time! The ground surface can't absorb that much water that quickly. Rivers and streams can't contain that much water, nor can the paved streets and sidewalks of a modern city.

For example, on July 7, 2012, a flash flood roared through the towns of Krasnodar Krai and Krymsk, Russia, with the force of a tsunami. Several months worth of rain—about 11 inches—fell on the region during the night. In the early hours of the morning, many homes, along with the people sleeping inside them, were swept away. More than 170 residents lost their lives. Another 13,000 were left homeless.

Other causes of flash flooding include the failure of dams, whether manmade or natural. One of the worst floods in United States history occurred on May 31, 1889, when the South Fork Dam on the Little Conemaugh River, 14 miles upstream from Johnstown, Pennsylvania, collapsed during a period of unusually heavy rainfall. With no advance warning, the residents of Johnstown were overwhelmed with more than 3,698 gallons of water. More than 2,000 people lost their lives and property damage was estimated at $17 million.[3]

Main Street in Johnstown, Pennsylvania, after the devastating flash flood due to dam failure, 1889

Flooding in Galena, Alaska, 2013

Naturally made dams can also collapse and wreak havoc on human environments. In spring, when snow and ice melt on the mountains, water rushes downhill, swelling rivers and streams. As the ice melts, large blocks of floating ice can collect on the river, creating dams that hold back tremendous amounts of water and ice. When the ice dam breaks, all that water and ice are suddenly released, sometimes with catastrophic results.

In early May 2009, the breakup of ice dams on the Yukon River in Alaska flooded the town of Eagle and virtually destroyed the Alaska Native settlement of Eagle Village. The freezing water of the Yukon River lifted homes and businesses right off their foundations. Huge blocks of floating ice smashed into whatever was left standing. Just four years later, ice dams on the Yukon River flooded the town of Galena, Alaska. A combination of floodwaters and ice blocks made streets impassable.

A slot canyon, such as this one in Kane, Utah, is a likely location for a flash flood.

credit: Shaan Hurley (CC BY 2.0)

DANGER IN THE CANYON

In the southwestern United States, dry streambeds, called arroyos, make great places to hike. Every year, thousands of outdoor enthusiasts visit sites such as the Grand Canyon in Arizona or Palo Duro Canyon State Park in Texas. But when flash floods occur in arroyos and steep-sided narrow canyons, they are especially dangerous. The weather can be clear skies and sunshine in one part of the canyon and pouring massive amounts of rain 20 or more miles upstream. All that water has to flow down.

Hikers caught unawares in the path of the resulting flash flood can neither outrun the torrent nor move out of its way.

Such was the case on July 31, 1976, when a stationary thunderstorm dropped 12 inches of rain over the upper levels of Big Thompson Canyon near Estes Park in Colorado. A wall of water 20 feet high raced down the canyon, claiming the lives of 143 people trapped in its path.

REGIONAL FLOODS

Flash floods claim more lives than regional floods, but it's the regional floods that tend to garner more of our attention. It's easy to see why. These floods almost invariably take place in large river valleys with low topography. When the rain falls for days or weeks at a time, we watch, spellbound by the unrelenting rise of the water.

A regional flood is a slower natural disaster than a flash flood. It allows people more time to move to higher, safer ground before they are swept away.

That's the good news. The bad news is that regional floods affect vast tracts of land and can impact the lives of millions. They can cause massive amounts of property damage, displace huge numbers of people, and leave a trail of disease in their wake.

Unusually heavy precipitation can result in regional flooding all on its own. Many other conditions contribute to the severity of a flood. We have already discussed two of those conditions in the 1931 floods in China. When unusual amounts of snow and ice pile up in the mountains, all that solid water turns to liquid during the spring thaw. The ground surface cannot absorb it all, the channel of the river cannot contain it all, and the conditions are set for flooding.

Prolonged droughts also increase the risk of flooding. When severe droughts are followed by sudden deluges, the excess water simply washes the soil away, sometimes resulting in dangerous mudslides.

If the ground freezes earlier than normal in fall or early winter, that, too, will increase the likelihood of flooding when warm weather returns in the spring. It takes time for the ground to absorb water. When it freezes, that absorption stops, essentially reducing the ground's absorption capacities when water levels increase during the spring.

This aerial photograph of a neighborhood in Santa Barbara, California, shows one result of what can happen when the ground surface cannot absorb all the precipitation falling from the sky. A mudslide has engulfed these houses.

credit: Staff Sgt. Cristian Meyers

When you think of the consequences of regional floods, your first thought may be of people drowning. In fact, however, relatively few people drown as a result of regional floods. All the same, these are true disasters with catastrophic effects. Floodwaters lift buildings off their foundations and carry them away. They wipe out streets, destroy bridges, and overwhelm sewage treatment facilities. When the waters recede, they leave homes and businesses mired in mud and saturated with water. These are perfect conditions for the growth of mold, which can lead to serious respiratory illnesses if not properly dealt with.

Widespread floods can lead to famine as well.

When large tracts of farmland lie submerged for weeks or months or when floods wipe out crops before they are harvested, millions of people can perish due to the resulting food shortages.

Waterborne illnesses are another potentially fatal result of regional floods. Floodwaters contaminated from overflowing sewage systems, industrial byproducts, or agricultural runoff seep into wells, making the water unsafe to drink. When victims of major floods cannot find access to an alternative water supply, they drink the contaminated water. They can contract diarrheal diseases such as typhoid fever and cholera.

DISASTER FACT

In 1995, flooding created widespread famine in North Korea. In one area, more than 30 inches of rain fell in the space of 72 hours. Just one inch of rainfall equals 22,650 gallons of water per acre of land. Thirty inches of rain produced an astonishing 679,500 gallons of water per acre! It wiped out huge tracts of farmland and grain reserves that had been stored underground.

A regional flood can leave homes and businesses, such as this gift shop, covered in mud.

Illnesses transmitted to humans by blood-feeding insects are yet another issue related to regional flooding. Outbreaks of malaria after flooding are especially dangerous. It may take weeks or months after the flood before the problem makes itself known. During that time, mosquitoes breeding in land covered with standing water can lead to widespread outbreaks of malaria. Malaria epidemics were reported after flooding in Costa Rica in 1991, for example, in the Dominican Republic in 2004, and in Sudan in 2013.

All of these health-related issues are further exacerbated if a regional flood displaces large numbers of people from their homes. Conditions are ripe for the spread of disease when flood refugees wind up living in makeshift camps or crowding into housing.

CONTROLLING THE RIVERS

What can we do about flooding? For nearly as long as human beings have lived near rivers, they have sought to control the flow of a river's water. The oldest-known dams were constructed by ancient Egyptians as far back as 2950 BCE.

Today, engineers take many different approaches to prevent rivers from overflowing their banks. They design technologically sophisticated dams. They construct enormous levees. They divert excess water through canals, guiding the water to large holding ponds or to natural areas that can absorb the water. They dredge river bottoms to increase the water-holding capacity of the river channel. Engineers widen the river's channel, change the course of the river itself, try to keep it clear of debris, and set up ever-more ingenious temporary barriers to hold back the water during actual floods.

FLOOD CONTROL IN THE NETHERLANDS

Few countries have more experience in flood control engineering than the Netherlands. The northern European country is located in a low-lying delta formed by the water runoff of three major rivers. One-third of the country sits below sea level and two-thirds of the country is at risk of flooding. Flood control is so important to the Dutch people it's written into their constitution that they have a right to be protected from floods!

For centuries, the Netherlands has engineered hard barriers, such as dams and dykes, to hold back floodwaters. Increasingly, however, Dutch engineers are finding ways to prevent floods by working with nature rather than against it. Now dykes and dams are being removed and space is being opened up to safely take in the floodwaters rather than to keep it out.[4]

VOCAB LAB

Write down what you think each word means. What root words can you find to help you? What does the context of the word tell you?

**drought,
dynamic equilibrium,
erosion, meanders,
precipitation,
sediment, tributary,**
and **water cycle**

Compare your definitions with those of your friends or classmates. Did you all come up with the same meanings? Turn to the text and glossary if you need help.

Levees, such as this one along the Sacramento River in California, are often made of earth piled up on a wide, level surface.

But rivers do not passively accept the changes we make to them. Rivers push back, always trying to maintain their natural equilibrium. Flood control is a process that never ends, partly because the changes we make feed directly into the negative feedback system that is part of the river's very existence.

While floodwaters can mean widespread death, damage, and disease, the natural disaster that could be considered water's opposite can also have devastating effects on people and land. In the next chapter, we'll take a closer—but not too close—look at wildfires.

KEY QUESTIONS

- **How is it possible for floods to take place even in arid areas such as deserts?**

- **Why is the death toll from a flash flood often higher than the death toll from a widespread regional flood?**

- **In what ways does the natural working of a river complicate the engineering challenges of flood control?**

IN YOUR OWN BACKYARD

What are the chances that a flash flood or regional flood will take place where you live? Using online resources and your own observations and knowledge about your town, assess the flood risk of your town.

- **Use the following questions to guide your research.**

  - What is the topography of your town? Do you live in the mountains, in a valley, or somewhere in between?

  - Are there rivers or streams where you live? If so, do they run close to homes and businesses?

  - Are there any dams on the rivers and/or streams where you live? What relevance might they have on a flood assessment?

  - Does your town have a history of flooding? If so, is it more prone to flash floods or regional floods?

  - What infrastructure would be affected by a flood in your area? Could major bridges get washed away? Where are sewage and water treatment facilities in your town located?

  - Where in your town can people find shelter if rising floodwaters force them out of their homes?

- **Now, create a visual presentation of your data and share it with classmates.** What questions do they have about flooding?

Explore navigation and flood control with the U.S. Army Corps of Engineers.

Navigation and Flood Control Mission

To investigate more, explore the work of the U.S. Army Corps of Engineers (USACE). The USACE employs more than 37,000 people and plays a major role in assessing flood risks and preventing floods. What are all those people doing?

FLOODS OF HISTORIC SIGNIFICANCE

All over the world, regional and flash floods have wreaked havoc on human populations. Research the story of a non-tsunami or storm surge-related flood that is of historic significance. Use the following questions to guide your inquiries. Create a written and/or visual presentation of your discoveries.

- **What kind of flood did you investigate—a flash flood or a regional flood?**

- **In what part of the world did this flood take place?**

- **What was the root cause of the flood?** What conditions made flooding possible?

- **What kind and how much damage did it cause?**

- **How many people did it affect?**

- **Were any steps taken afterward to prevent flooding in the future?** If so, have those efforts been successful? Why or why not?

To investigate more, do an internet exploration of the flood-control measures currently underway in Japan. Japanese engineers have come up with some of the most innovative ways to protect their island nation from its long history of flooding.

Chapter 6
Wildfires: Out of Control

How can something we seem to have so much control over cause so much damage?

Though we might think we control fire, in reality, once a fire escapes our sphere of influence, it has the power to go wherever it's driven by the right conditions.

In the summer of 2018, much of Europe experienced a prolonged heat wave. Little rain and high temperatures left vegetation throughout the continent dried out and unusually combustible. In Athens, Greece, this continent-wide weather pattern combined with two sparks that created one of the deadliest wildfire events in the twenty-first century.

On July 23, 2018, two fires started almost simultaneously—one near the beach town of Kineta, on the western side of Athens, and the other near Penteli, about 33 miles away on the northern side of Athens. In both locations, strong winds pushed the wildfires across the parched landscape with speeds that reached upward of 77 miles per hour.

In some instances, flames were so intense that people burned to death inside their houses and cars before they could even formulate an escape route. Others ran toward the beach and the hoped-for safety of the water only to be burned in their tracks, mere steps away from the ocean.

The mystery of what set off this natural disaster remains unsolved. Some say the fires were started by a spark created by a damaged cable on a utility pole. Others say it was an act of arson.

Either way, the Athens fires of 2018 claimed the lives of at least 100 people and prompted more than two dozen countries to assist Greece in fighting the fires and recovering from the disaster.

We humans have learned to create fire virtually at will. We flick a lighter, strike a match, turn the switch on a gas-powered fireplace—and just like that, fire appears. We seem to have control over it.

But fire is a natural force, similar to water or wind. And like all forces of nature, fire can be challenging to harness for our own purposes.

These 2009 wildfires in Greece were captured by satellite

credit: NASA image courtesy Jeff Schmaltz, MODIS Rapid Response at NASA GSFC

This residential neighborhood in Yorba Linda, California, was ravaged by a wildfire in 2008.

If a wildfire races toward our home or business, the only "control" we may have is to get out of its way as quickly as possible. In today's world, wildfires increasingly cross the boundary that separates nature from civilization. We are frequently reminded of the true character of fire in the natural order of our world. Let's take a closer look.

FIRE TO THE RESCUE

Have you ever walked through a forest and realized how many fallen leaves were at your feet? Those leaves are just a small amount of the organic material that plants produce in staggering quantities.

Branches, leaves, trees, flowers, vegetables, grass, pine needles, vines—it all piles up! But where does all that organic plant material go?

In a suburban neighborhood, sanitation crews might haul it all off to a local landfill, or shred it to be used as mulch for gardening purposes. Out in rural areas, a lot of that plant material gets recycled through decomposition and digestion—material rots on the ground or is consumed by animals and returned into the ecosystem as bodily waste.

Decomposition and digestion alone can't always control all of that vegetation. In fact, there are places where the accumulation is so great that it threatens the health of the natural environment. In a crowded ecosystem, plants compete for vital resources—nutrients in the soil, water, and sunlight, for example.

If overcrowding is not controlled, the strain on those resources can be severe enough to wipe out the entire plant community. There simply won't be enough to go around.

Fortunately, a natural recycling program has evolved to deal with this very problem—wildfires. In what are known as fire-dependent ecosystems, an occasional wildfire sweeps through the area and burns out some of the excess vegetation.

The dead plant material decomposes more quickly. Nutrients are returned to the soil, more water and sunlight are available to the surviving plants, and the plant community regenerates itself.

Large swaths of the natural world depend on this process to maintain healthy ecosystems.

LET IT BURN!

The U.S. Forest Service is the government agency that protects and maintains millions of acres of private and public forest in the United States. Founded in 1905, the agency's approach to wildfires has evolved dramatically. Prior to the 1960s, the agency's goal was one of total suppression. All wildfires were to be prevented, and those that couldn't be prevented were to be extinguished as soon as possible. But as ecologists began to understand the many benefits that wildfires bring to ecosystems, the Forest Service revised its approach. Now, if property and human lives are not endangered, wildfires are allowed to follow their natural course. Explore the impact of Smokey Bear through these two website!

 legend Smokey Bear

 Eddy Arnold Smokey 1952

The grasslands in Africa, such as this one in the Masai Mara National Park in Kenya, are ecosystems that depend on wildfires to maintain the health of the plant community.

credit: Key45 (CC BY 2.0)

Fire-dependent ecosystems, such as grasslands, can be found on the African veldts, the pampas of South America, the steppes of Eurasia, and the plains of North America.

Fire-dependent ecosystems also exist in temperate forests around the world, in countries such as Japan, China, the United States, and parts of Russia.

They are also located in five Mediterranean climate zones, including the Mediterranean basin, California, central Chile, southwest Australia, the Cape Province of South Africa, and the southeastern tip of Vancouver Island, Canada.

PHOTOSYNTHESIS IN REVERSE

We have a standard definition for fire. It is a rapid combination of carbon, oxygen, hydrogen, and organic material that produces flame, heat, and light. But there's another way to think about fire—photosynthesis in reverse.

What does that mean? Photosynthesis is the process by which plants use carbon, oxygen, water, and sunlight to produce vegetation. Plants harvest energy from the sun and store it as cellulose in their branches, leaves, and flowers.

Remember the First Law of Thermodynamics: Energy is neither created nor destroyed. When a tree catches on fire, that stored solar energy is returned to the atmosphere as heat—photosynthesis in reverse!

Look at the chemical equation for photosynthesis side by side with the chemical equation for fire. Do you see how the two processes are mirror images of one another?

Chemical equation for photosynthesis

$$6CO_2 + 6H_2O + sunlight >>> C_6H_{12}O_6 + 6O_2$$

Chemical Equation for fire[1]

$$C_2H_{12}O_6 + 6O_2 >>> 6CO_2 + 6H_2O + released\ heat$$

THE FIRE TETRAHEDRON

Experts think of the requirements for fire as a tetrahedron shape. The three ingredients of fire are as follows.

* First, fire needs oxygen, an element that makes up 21 percent of Earth's atmosphere. In most natural settings, there is almost always enough oxygen to at least get a fire started.

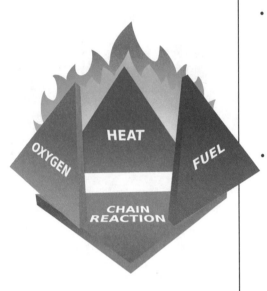

- Second, fire needs heat. This ingredient is harder to come by than oxygen. Many plant materials, such as wood, remain stable up to temperatures as high as 480 degrees Fahrenheit (249 degrees Celsius). So it takes something quite hot to get a fire started. In nature, that spark most often is provided by lightning.

- The third ingredient is fuel, which can be any kind of combustible material—something that can catch on fire. It can be nearly anything, from a couch cushion to a piece of dryer lint. But in a wildfire, the fire feeds primarily on grasses, shrubs, trees, and slash. This is organic debris on the ground following storms or logging, and, with increasing frequency, houses.

- The fourth requirement is the chemical reaction itself, which needs to happen in order for the fire to start from these three ingredients.

A bolt of lightning can hit combustible materials, such as trees, with more than 100 times the amount of heat required to ignite a flame.

FIRE AS A NATURAL DISASTER

All the heat and oxygen in the world cannot make a fire without fuel. And it is the presence (or absence) of fuel, combined with the presence (or absence) of human beings, which largely determines whether a wildfire becomes a natural disaster.

If a bolt of lightning sparks a fire in an uninhabited area of the African veldt, for example, the resulting wildfire probably will not develop into a natural disaster. If lightning sparks a flame among some dry shrubs in a forested area close to a Los Angeles suburb, however, there's a much greater chance that a natural disaster will occur.

Dry conditions in the forest provide the fire with ample fuel to spread beyond the natural setting, leading straight to the doors of homes and businesses.

> And contemporary, manmade structures provide wildfires with a feast of combustible materials.

An out-of-control wildfire can result in an enormous loss of both public and private land, millions of dollars in property damages, and loss of human life.

FUEL FOR THE FIRE

Fires begin and grow where there is available fuel. That might be grass in an American prairie, trees in a Russian forest, shrubs along an Italian hillside, or a home in the path of a fire burning through a residential community in the United States.

HOW FIRES SPREAD

No two wildfires are the same. One may move slowly along the ground. Another may march through a landscape as a wall of fire moving along a flaming combustion front. Still another may take the form of a crown fire, racing through the tops of trees.

But all wildfires are affected by a combination of four factors:

- The type and quantity of available fuel
- Weather patterns, especially wind
- The shape of the land, called the topography
- Behavior within the fire itself

But not all fuels are created equal. Some will ignite easier and burn faster than others. Oil is a highly combustible material, so a shrub with low oil content is naturally less "fire friendly" than a shrub with high oil content.

That's what makes eucalyptus trees in California a controversial topic today.

Native to Australia, eucalyptus trees were introduced to California in 1850 by Australians coming to the state to take part in the famous California Gold Rush. Eucalyptus trees have very high oil content and, more than 150 years later, they populate the California landscape by the tens of thousands.

Some people argue that the eucalyptus trees are a fire hazard. They want as many as possible to be ripped out and replaced with less combustible trees, such as live oaks. Others contend that the eucalyptus trees are an important part of California culture. They want the trees to stay, even if they present a fire hazard. Who do you think is right?

Water content also plays an important role in determining how fire friendly a combustible material is. Waterlogged plants are harder to set on fire and harder to keep burning than dry, dead vegetation.

The sizes and shapes of fuel sources are important factors as well. When we think of wildfires, we often imagine tall trees going up in flames. That certainly happens.

Read about the eucalyptus in California and hear some of the voices in the debate in this article.

KQED
eucalyptus

Eucalyptus trees in the Bay area

credit: Peter Alfred Hess (CC BY 2.0)

But low shrubs (bushes from 2 to 12 feet tall) make an excellent fuel, too. Their loose layering allows for the free flow of oxygen, and they can have high oil content as well.

If you see a stately Douglas fir tree on fire, it may have been a humble snowberry shrub underneath it that provided the fuel and oxygen that the fire needed to climb its way up the tree.

Then there are the types of buildings we live in. If a wildfire comes knocking on the doors of a neighborhood where the houses are made of wood with wood shingles on their roofs, those homes will add fuel to the fire. If a wildfire runs into a neighborhood filled with cement, brick, or stucco houses with ceramic or slate tiles on their roofs, it's not going to find a readily available fuel source.

The Rim Fire in the Stanislaus National Forest near in California in 2013

credit: U.S. Department of Agriculture

WHAT IS AIR PRESSURE?

Air pressure is the weight of air molecules pressing in at any given point on Earth. If you stand next to the ocean, that air pressure amounts to about 15 pounds per square inch, pressing in on you and everything else in sight. Air pressure is always highest near sea level. As you climb to higher elevations, you have fewer air molecules weighing you down. If you blew up a balloon at sea level, for example, and immediately carried it to the top of a mountain, the balloon would get bigger. Did more air seep inside the balloon? No. But on the mountaintop, there is less air pressure squeezing on the balloon from the outside. This allows the air inside the balloon to expand, and it will continue to expand until it equals the air pressure around it.

WEATHER AND WIND

Weather plays an important role in the life of a wildfire. If it's been raining for a month and vegetation is full of water, even a lightning bolt may have a hard time starting a fire.

Just the opposite is true, of course, during periods of drought. If combustible organic plant materials are dried out or dead, it will take much less than a 50,000 degree Fahrenheit (27,760 degree Celsius) lightning bolt to start a fire. An ember from a dying campfire, a dropped cigarette, sparks flying off a car as it zooms down a paved road while dragging its muffler—all these little things, and more, can lead to a raging inferno.

> Wind, more than any other weather phenomenon, however, most directly affects the course a wildfire will take.

You know wind when you feel it blowing hair in your face or making you button up your coat on a blustery day. But do you know what wind actually is? Do you know where wind comes from?

Whether it's a gentle breeze or a stiff gust, wind is air that is moving. And what moves air around are differences in air pressure caused primarily by heat and water vapor. Air that's under lots of pressure naturally moves toward areas with less pressure. The greater the difference between high pressure and low pressure, the faster the air will move.

Imagine a warm breeze coming in off the ocean on a hot summer day. Heat from the sun is warming the water, which warms the air above it, causing it to rise. The rising warm air leaves behind an area of low pressure.

Air from the land, which is now at a higher pressure than the air over the water, rushes in to fill the space. That rushing air? That's wind!

There are ordinary winds, and then there are dry, hot winds called Foehn winds. Where wildfires are concerned, Foehn winds are the ones we want to pay attention to.

> Foehn winds are large, regional winds that form as air travels up and around mountains.

As air rises up the side of a mountain, it expands and cools due to the decrease in air pressure. Cold air holds less water vapor than warm air, so the moisture condenses, forms clouds, and causes either rain or snow to fall above the mountain's upwind slope. As the water molecules change from a vapor to a liquid, latent energy is released, heating the mountain air. As precipitation falls away, warm, dry air remains, and then blows down the other side of the mountain.

Foehn winds

FOEHN WINDS NEAR AND FAR

Foehn winds behave the same way wherever they occur, but throughout the world they are known by many different names. South Africans might call them the Bergwinds. Folks in Southern California know them as the Santa Anna winds. Those along the Pacific coast call them the Diablo winds. In the Rocky Mountains, they are named Chinook. In China, the name is Wuhan. Same weather event, different name.

DISASTER FACT

Fire always proceeds faster up a slope than over the ground.

Foehn winds don't happen all the time, however. They require a stagnant block of high air pressure on the leeward side of a mountain. When that happens, the difference between high and low air pressure is great, causing the warm air to flow very fast—anywhere from 40 to 60 miles per hour—with gusts up to 100 miles per hour.

Foehn winds also raise surface temperatures quickly and dramatically. They can increase surface temperatures by 36 degrees Fahrenheit (2 degrees Celsius) within minutes, while simultaneously lowering humidity levels in equally dramatic fashion.

How long do Foehn winds blow? Sometimes, they last for less than an hour. Other times, they last for days. Either way, if they happen to be blowing when a spark catches fire in a dry patch of scrub, there's a good chance a fire will start. And the longer the Foehn winds blow, the more likely it is that the fire will develop into a hard-to-control wildfire.

TOPOGRAPHY

The lay of the land and the type of vegetation growing on it will either hinder or assist in the spread of fire. The most significant topographical feature, however, is slope. Fire typically travels faster up a hill than it does down a hill. In general, the steeper the slope, the faster the fire will move. Why is that?

Remember, wind is generated by air moving from an area of high pressure to an area of low pressure—from lower to higher elevations. So, winds flow uphill and push the fire on its way. Also, heat and smoke rising up ahead of the fire itself preheat the fuel in the fire's path, making it even easier for the fire to continue its march up the hill.

Once fire reaches the top of a hill, it will have a harder time progressing down the other side.

Any winds will probably be blowing against it, and it can no longer preheat the fuel it needs to survive.

THE PERSONALITY OF FIRE

Wildfires are acted upon by such a variety of unpredictable forces that no two wildfires can be said to be alike. Within their many differences, however, wildfires can share some similarities in the particular form that their destruction takes.

If the blaze from a wildfire is intense enough, for example, the clouds of smoke it creates can spawn dangerous thunderstorms that result in lightning and rain. This is what happened in a May 2018 wildfire southeast of Amarillo, Texas. A large pyrocumulus cloud, also called a fire cloud, formed, which created a severe thunderstorm north of the actual fire.

Watch some video footage of wildfires and learn more about how they start.

Nat Geo wildfires 101

A pyrocumulus cloud from the Station Fire in the La Cañada Flintridge region of Los Angeles, 2009

credit: EllsworthC (CC BY 3.0)

An Epic Forest Fire

The deadliest forest fire in U.S. history took place in Peshtigo, Wisconsin, on October 8, 1871. At that time, it was standard practice to clear forestland for farms by setting controlled fires. On that particular day, unusually strong winds blew in on a cold front and fanned the many small fires into a catastrophic conflagration. By the time the fire died out, more than 1.2 million acres of forest had burned and an estimated 1,500 to 2,500 people lost their lives. There were not enough people left alive in the rural community to identify all the bodies. A plaque marks the spot of a mass grave for the hundreds of victims.

Wildfires can also create so-called fire tornadoes. These are not real tornadoes, of course, which form from super cells of warm, moist air, but they certainly look like flaming versions of real tornadoes! They tend to be of short duration, since they rapidly run out of fuel. But, during their brief lifespans, fire tornadoes can reach temperatures of 2,000 degrees Fahrenheit (1,093 degrees Celsius) and move very quickly. They can cause a lot of damage in a short amount of time.[2]

Large wildfires can also create their own wind patterns. So, even if no local or regional winds are spreading the flames, the scorching air of the fire itself sets the air around it in motion. The resulting winds carry burning embers away from the original location of the fire and start new fires of their own in distant places.

In the United States, the vast majority of wildfires are caused by human beings. A very few of these fires are started by arsonists, people who deliberately set fires. Most, however, are the result of accidents.

Here are some steps all of us can take to prevent those accidents from happening.

- Thoroughly extinguish all campfires by dousing them with water and stirring the embers until they are cool.

- When you burn debris or household trash, always have a shovel and some water on hand in case the flames get out of control. Never burn debris during windy conditions.

- Dispose of cigarettes and matches properly. Do not toss lit cigarettes or matches on the ground or out automobile windows.

- Never leave a fire unattended.

- Call 911 if you see an unattended or out-of-control fire.

The natural processes that make Earth home for a multitude of life forms are complex, mysterious, beautiful, and—sometimes—powerful almost beyond comprehension. Most of the time, those powerful forces maintain and regenerate our planet without causing any harm to us human beings.

Every now and again, however, nature runs roughshod over everything people hold near and dear. The ground shakes and collapses our buildings. Molten lava explodes and poisons our air. The winds roar and capsize our ships. A whirling storm rips the roofs off our schools. The rivers overflow their banks and drown our crops. Fire consumes our homes.

Those are natural disasters, all examples of nature colliding with humanity.

KEY QUESTIONS

- **How do naturally occurring wildfires have a positive effect on an ecosystem?**

- **What three elements are required for fire to survive? Can you think of some ways to deprive a fire of one to three of the elements it needs to keep burning?**

- **Why does a wildfire move faster up a hill than down it?**

VOCAB LAB

Write down what you think each word means. What root words can you find to help you? What does the context of the word tell you?

combustible, conflagration, decomposition, fire-dependent ecosystem, Foehn winds, nutrients, organic, photosynthesis, topography, and **wildfire**.

Compare your definitions with those of your friends or classmates. Did you all come up with the same meanings? Turn to the text and glossary if you need help.

Inquire & Investigate

View film footage of some of the wildfires that swept across Europe in 2017.

BBC News Southern Italy wildfire

To investigate more, compare and contrast the wildfires of 2017 and 2018. There were about 13,000 fewer wildfires worldwide in 2018. Why? What was different? Where and when did these fires take place?

WORLD ON FIRE

The year 2017 was one of the worst years for wildfires in the recorded history of our planet. From the United States to Russia, South America, Canada, and Europe, much of the world was on fire. Let's take a look at why.

• **Investigate the causes and consequences of the worldwide phenomenon of wildfires in the year 2017 and create a written and/or visual presentation of your discoveries.** The following questions can help guide your research.

- In addition to the United States, can you name five other countries that were hard hit by wildfires in 2017?

- What were at least two main causes behind the increase in wildfires in 2017?

- What role did climate change play in creating conditions favorable to a worldwide explosion in both the number and the severity of wildfires in 2017?

- Why did some people say that wildfires in 2017 were happening "in the wrong parts of the world"?

- Can you gather enough figures to estimate how many acres were burned worldwide due to wildfires in 2017? In dollar figures, how much property damage did wildfires cause? How many lives were lost?

- Has the scientific community determined whether the increase of wildfires in 2017 was a one-time event or do they expect similarly severe fire seasons to occur again in the near future?

FIGHTING WILDFIRES

The principle behind fighting wildfires never changes. If you can remove just one element of the Fire Triangle—be it heat, fuel, or oxygen—the fire will go out. But how exactly do we fight wildfires today, when they rage across millions of acres of land and sweep through highly populated neighborhoods in all four corners of the globe?

- **Research the subject of modern wildfire fighting techniques.** The following questions may help guide your investigations.

  - How many ways do firefighters try to remove oxygen from the Fire Triangle?

  - How many ways do they try to remove fuel from the Fire Triangle?

  - How many ways do they try to remove heat from the Fire Triangle?

- **Create a written and/or visual presentation of what you discover.** Can you think of innovative ways of helping prevent forest fires?

> **To investigate more,** look into the ways that architects and engineers are designing fireproof buildings for both residential and business purposes.

Meet the men and women who fought wildfires in British Columbia in 2017.

firefighters
B.C.'s wildfires

GLOSSARY

accelerating: increasing in speed.

adjacent: next to or adjoining something else.

adverse: harmful, unfortunate.

aftershock: a smaller earthquake that occurs after a major earthquake.

air pressure: the force of the gases surrounding the earth pressing downward, sometimes called barometric pressure.

amplify: cause to become greater in number or more intense.

amplitude: the height of a wave.

andesitic magma: a relatively thick magma with a high silicon-oxygen content.

anemometer: an instrument that measures wind speed.

aptly: describes something done in an appropriate manner.

arroyo: a dry, steep sided gully that was formed by fast-flowing water.

arson: the act of deliberately setting a fire.

asthenosphere: the semisolid, plastic layer of Earth located beneath the rigid upper lithosphere.

atmosphere: the envelope of gases that surround a planet.

atomic: having to do with atoms, the tiny particles of matter that make up everything.

avalanche: a sudden and quick downhill flow of snow and ice from a mountain.

aviary: a large building or enclosure for keeping birds.

basaltic magma: a relatively thin magma that flows easily.

bisect: cut in half.

body waves: seismic waves that travel through the interior of Earth.

buoyant: inclined to stay afloat.

capsize: to tip over.

carbon: an element that is found in all life on Earth and in coal, petroleum, and diamonds.

carbonated: describes a fizzy soft drink that contains dissolved carbon dioxide.

cellulose: the main substance found in vegetable matter, such as plants and trees.

chemical bond: the attraction of atoms that binds chemical substances together.

chemistry: the science of how substances interact, combine, and change.

classification: to systematically arrange items into groups based on common features these items have.

colossal: huge.

combustible: capable of burning.

comprehension: understanding.

compression waves: waves that are pushed together by the medium through which they travel.

condensation: the changing of a gas into a liquid, such as when water vapor becomes liquid water.

conduit: a channel that conveys fluid.

conflagration: an out-of-control fire.

contaminate: to make something impure.

continental crust: the section of Earth's crust that is located on the continental landmasses.

continental drift: the scientific theory that the continents are in motion.

contour: an outline that forms the shape of something.

convection: air that is constantly circulating.

core: the deepest level of interior Earth.

Coriolis effect: the spinning movement that Earth makes as it rotates on its axis and the way it deflects circulating air.

crater: a large, bowl-shaped cavity generally located at the top of a volcano.

crops: plants grown for food and other uses.

crust: the outermost layer of Earth.

current: the flow of water or air in one direction.

cyclone: hurricane.

dam: a natural or manmade barrier to flowing water.

decomposition: the decay of vegetable matter.

digestion: the mechanical and chemical process by which a living organism breaks down food so it can be used to fuel the body.

Doppler radar: a type of radar used to locate precipitation, calculate its motion, and determine its type.

dormant: at rest; no longer active.

downdraft: a downward moving current of air.

drought: a long period of time with little or no rain.

dynamic equilibrium: descriptive of a system that reacts to change so that it maintains a balanced state.

dynamic: characterized by change.

earthquake: a sudden, sometimes violent, shaking of the ground caused by seismic activity.

ecosystem: a biological community made up of all the living organisms in that one area.

electromagnetic spectrum: the range of wavelengths or frequencies over which electromagnetic radiation extends.

elongate: to make something longer, especially in relation to its width.

engineer: a person who uses science, math, and creativity to design and build things.

epicenter: the point on the surface of Earth directly above the hypocenter of an earthquake.

epidemic: a widespread occurrence of an infectious disease.

equilibrium: a state of balance.

erosion: the process of sediment being picked up in one place and deposited in another.

eruption: a violent explosion of gas, steam, or ash.

eruption column: a cloud of superheated gas emitted from a volcano during a violent eruption.

evacuation: the act of leaving an area due to an approaching natural disaster, such as a hurricane.

evaporation: the process of a liquid heating up and becoming a gas.

evolve: to change through time.

extinction event: an event that causes a species to die out.

eye wall: a ring of severe thunderstorms just outside the eye of a hurricane.

eye: the calm center section of a hurricane.

famine: a widespread and long-term lack of food that can lead to starvation.

fault block mountain: a mountain that forms by tectonic plates rising and/or falling in relation to one another.

fault line: a fracture in Earth's crust as the result of an earthquake.

fault plane: the flat surface along which there is a slip between tectonic plates during an earthquake.

fire-dependent ecosystem: an ecosystem that needs the occasional wildfire to sweep through to control an overabundance of vegetation.

firestorm: a fire that is so large and intense it creates and sustains its own weather system.

fissure: a split or crack that creates a long, narrow opening.

flank: the side of a volcano.

flash flood: a sudden and short-lived flood caused by such things as thunderstorms or broken dams.

flood: when water covers an area that is usually dry.

focus: the point where an earthquake originates, also known as the hypocenter.

Foehn winds: large regional winds that form as air travels up and around mountains.

fold mountain: a mountain that forms when one tectonic plate rides over another and one plate buckles and folds.

forecast: to predict what the weather will be like in the future.

fuel: any material that provides energy.

Fujita scale: the scientific measurement of the amount of damage that a tornado causes.

funnel: a tube or pipe that is wide at the top and narrow at the bottom.

geological disaster: natural disasters that include avalanches, landslides, earthquakes, sinkholes, and volcanic eruptions.

geology: the science of Earth's physical structures, the materials that make up Earth, and the processes that act upon them. A geologist studies geology.

global warming: an increase in the earth's average temperatures, enough to cause climate change.

gradient: slope.

GLOSSARY

grassland: a large open area of land covered with grasses.

habitation: a particular place where living organisms exist.

hazard: a danger.

heat capacity: the degree to which a substance can absorb heat.

homo sapiens: the species to which all modern human beings belong.

hospitable: favorable for living.

humid: a weather condition marked by large amounts of water vapor in the atmosphere.

hurricane: a tropical storm with sustained winds of at least 74 miles per hour and a definite rotation around a central point.

hydrological disaster: water-related natural disasters, including floods and tsunamis.

hydrology: the science of Earth's water, especially its movement in relation to land. A hydrologist studies hydrology.

hypocenter: the point where an earthquake originates.

inertia: a tendency to do nothing and/or to remain unchanged.

influx: an arrival of a large number or amount of something.

inundate: flood.

irrigation: the supply of water to land or crops.

jet stream: a narrow band of strong westerly winds that circle the globe several miles above the surface of Earth.

landslide: the sudden sliding down of a mass of land or rock from a mountain or cliff.

latent: existing but not yet developed or capable of being used.

lava: molten or semi-fluid rock that erupts from a volcano.

leeward: the side that doesn't get hit by the traveling winds.

levee: a natural or manmade structure that stops water from going where we don't want it to go.

limnic eruption: when carbon dioxide suddenly erupts from deep lake waters and forms a gas cloud.

lithosphere: the rigid outer section of Earth.

Love waves: seismic surface waves that vibrate perpendicular to Earth's surface.

low pressure: an area in the atmosphere where the air pressure is lower than the surrounding air.

magma: hot, melted rock.

magma chamber: a large reservoir of liquid rock.

mandatory: something that is required.

mantle: the thickest part of Earth's interior.

mass extinction events: events that result in the widespread destruction of life.

meanders: river bends.

meteor: an object, such as an asteroid, that burns and vaporizes when it enters Earth's atmosphere.

meteorological disaster: weather-related natural disasters, including blizzards, droughts, thunderstorms, hurricanes, hailstorms, heat waves, and tornadoes.

meteorology: the study of weather and climate. A meteorologist studies meteorology and forecasts the weather.

molten rock: rock that has melted.

Moment Magnitude Scale: the measurement of the size of an earthquake.

mudslide: a mass of mud that has fallen down a hillside.

natural disaster: a natural event, such as a fire or flood, that causes great damage.

negative feedback loop: describes any system that reacts to change in a way that seeks to return the system to its original state.

nutrients: substances that provide nourishment.

oasis: a calm and safe place.

oceanic crust: the section of Earth's crust that is located on the floor of ocean basins.

organic: relating to living matter.

organism: a living thing, such as a plant or animal.

oversaturated: the condition of ground having more water than it can absorb.

Pangaea: the supercontinent that once contained all the landmass of Earth.

parallel: describes objects that run side by side and have an unchanging distance between them.

perpendicular: describes an object that is situated at a 90-degree angle in relation to a given plane or surface.

phenomenon: a remarkable event.

photosynthesis: the process by which plants use carbon, oxygen, water, and sunlight to produce vegetation.

physics: the scientific study of the nature and properties of matter and energy.

plastic: able to be molded.

pliable: describes a material that can be molded or reshaped.

positive feedback loop: a system where any change provokes a response that seeks to enhance the change.

precipitation: rain, hail, snow, or sleet produced from clouds.

projectile: an object that is thrown at high speed through the air.

prolong: to keep something going.

pyroclastic flows: enormous clouds of gas and ash released by a volcano during an eruption.

quantitative: measured by the quantity, or number, of something rather than the quality.

radiation: energy transmitted in the form of rays, waves, or particles from a source, such as the sun.

radioactive: to emit energy in the form of particles or radiation.

radiosonde: an instrument carried by weather balloons to measure various aspects of the atmosphere.

rain bands: the outer section of a hurricane, made up of dense, spiraling clouds.

Rayleigh waves: surface seismic waves that travel in backward rotating circles.

regulate: to control or supervise something.

rhyolitic magma: a very thick magma with a relatively high silicon-oxygen content.

Richter scale: a scale used to measure the size of an earthquake.

Ring of Fire: a large stretch of the Pacific Ocean where many earthquakes take place and where many volcanoes are located.

rural: having to do with a country setting, as opposed to a city or urban area.

safeguard: to protect.

saturated: soaked with liquid.

sediment: dirt and organic matter that is carried by erosion from one spot in a river to another.

seismic: related to earthquakes.

seismic waves: the form that released energy takes when an earthquake occurs.

seismograph: an instrument that measures and records earthquake activity.

shear waves: the second wave that follows after an earthquake; also called an S-wave, it is a wave that moves through the earth rather than on the surface.

shoaling effect: the effect that shallow water plays in creating larger waves as they approach land from the deep ocean.

simultaneously: happening at the same time.

sinkhole: a hole in the ground caused by water erosion.

sinuous: winding or curvy, like a snake.

slope: a rising or falling surface, such as a hillside.

soil liquefaction: the process of solid earth being shaken to the point where it behaves as if it were a liquid.

space disaster: a natural disaster caused by something that originates in space.

species: a group of plants or animals that are closely related and produce offspring.

speculate: to form a theory without firm evidence to support it.

stagnant: not moving; having no current or flow.

storm surge: the sea water pushed along by a hurricane. It rushes inland and causes flooding when the storm reaches the coastline.

stratosphere: the layer of Earth's atmosphere that extends about 32 miles above the surface of the planet.

stucco: plaster-coated walls.

subside: to become less intense or severe; with water, to return to normal levels.

suburban: a residential district outside a city.

suppression: the act of keeping something from happening; holding something down.

surface waves: seismic waves that travel across the surface of Earth's crust.

technology: the tools, methods, and systems used to solve a problem or do work.

GLOSSARY

tectonic plates: sections of Earth's crust that move atop the semisolid layer of Earth known as the asthenosphere.

tetrahedron: a pyramid containing four triangular faces.

timberland: land covered with trees that can be harvested for wood.

topography: the physical features of a natural environment.

tornado: a violent, twisting, funnel-shaped column of air extending from a thunderstorm to the ground.

torrential: falling rapidly and in vast quantities.

toxic: poisonous.

trajectory: the path followed by a projectile or by an object being acted on by outside forces.

tributary: a smaller body of water that connects to a larger river.

tropical depression: the second stage of a hurricane: a storm marked as a collection of thunderstorms with sustained winds of 23 to 39 miles per hour.

tropical disturbance: the first stage of a hurricane; a storm marked by a mass of individual thunderstorms with only slight winds.

tropical storm: the third stage of a hurricane; a storm with a circular shape that reaches maximum sustained winds of between 39 and 73 miles per hour.

troposphere: the layer of the atmosphere that is closest to Earth's surface.

tsunami: a large wave created by the energy released during an earthquake that takes place on an ocean floor.

turbulent: moving unsteadily or violently.

typhoon: the name for a hurricane over the western Pacific Ocean.

ubiquitous: occurring in all places.

unfathomable: not capable of being understood.

uninhabitable: unsuitable to life.

unsanitary: not clean; dirty.

updraft: an upward moving current of air.

vacuum: an empty space; a space entirely devoid of matter.

vaporization: the act of a liquid becoming a gas, such as when water turns into water vapor.

velocity: the speed of something moving in one direction.

vent: an opening that allows air, gas, or liquid to escape a confined space.

viscosity: the relative thickness of a liquid substance.

viscous: how thick a liquid substance is.

vital: necessary to existence.

volatile: unstable and/or dangerous.

volcanic: from lava that came out of a volcano.

volcanic mountain: a mountain that forms as a result of volcanic activity.

volcano: a vent in the earth's surface through which magma, ash, and gases erupt.

volcanologist: a scientist who studies volcanoes.

vortex: a whirlpool or whirlwind.

wake: a trail of something left behind.

water cycle: the continuous movement of water from the earth to the clouds and back to Earth again.

water vapor: the gas form of water.

wave length: the distance between waves.

wildfire: a large, destructive fire that spreads out of control.

METRIC CONVERSIONS

Use this chart to find the metric equivalents to the English measurements in this activity. If you need to know a half measurement, divide by two. If you need to know twice the measurement, multiply by two.

ENGLISH	METRIC	
1 inch	2.5	centimeters
1 foot	30.5	centimeters
1 yard	0.9	meter
1 mile	1.6	kilometers
1 pound	0.5	kilogram
1 teaspoon	5	milliliters
1 tablespoon	15	milliliters
1 cup	237	milliliters

BOOKS

Ferguson, Gary. *Land on Fire: The New Reality of Wildfire in the West.* Timber Press, 2017.

Fountain, Henry. *The Great Quake: How the Biggest Earthquake in North America Changed Our Understanding of the Planet.* Crown, 2017.

Hargrove, Brantley. *The Man Who Caught the Storm: The Life of Legendary Tornado Chaser Tim Samaras.* Simon & Schuster, 2018.

Jones, Lucy. *The Big Ones: How Natural Disasters Have Shaped Us (And What We Can Do About Them).* Doubleday, 2018.

Larson, Erik. *Isaac's Storm: A Man, a Time, and the Deadliest Hurricane in History.* Vintage, 2010.

McCullough, David. *The Johnstown Flood.* Simon & Schuster, 1987.

Scotti, R.A. *Sudden Sea: The Great Hurricane of 1938.* Back Bay Books, 2004.

Winchester, Simon. *Krakatoa: The Day the World Exploded: August 27, 1883.* Harper Perennial, 2005.

VIDEOS

The Big Burn: The Largest Fire in American History. PBS.

Krakatoa: The Great Volcanic Eruption. 2005.

National Geographic: Top 10 Natural Disasters. BBC.

Perfect Storms: God's Wrath. Smithsonian Channel.

Perfect Storms: The Great Galveston Hurricane. Smithsonian Channel.

The Wrath of God: Flash Floods—Deadly Downpour. History Channel.

MUSEUMS

Johnstown Flood Museum, Johnstown, Pennsylvania:
jaha.org

The Watersnoodmuseum, Ouwerkerk, Netherlands:
watersnoodmuseum.nl/en/the-museum

RESOURCES

QR CODE GLOSSARY

page 5: theweathernetwork.com/news/articles/
watch-the-african-lake-that-could-explode-with-deadly-gas/65320

page 19: theguardian.com/world/live/2016/nov/16/
new-zealand-earthquake-help-stranded-kaikoura-live

page 22: nationalgeographic.org/thisday/apr18/great-san-francisco-earthquake

page 31: youtube.com/watch?v=v2pPRiUUnOg

page 38: youtube.com/watch?v=ghl33n26d44

page 40: volcano.si.edu/reports_weekly.cfm

page 40: wovo.org/observatories

page 48: youtube.com/watch?v=11pjSTnl99Q

page 51: youtube.com/watch?v=evxGkUFpV54&feature=youtu.be

page 52: youtube.com/watch?v=a-SnxC-BkPo

page 56: newsweek.com/scientists-are-planning-stop-hurricanes-their-tracks-blowing-air-bubbles-sea-855623

page 57: youtube.com/watch?v=Grziaq-caVE

page 58: commons.wikimedia.org/wiki/File:Wea00920.jpg

page 62: youtube.com/watch?v=7KDz6dGQ5RE

page 65: youtube.com/watch?v=FmnkQ2ytlO8

page 66: commons.wikimedia.org/wiki/File:NWS_2013_Moore_radar_loop.gif

page 76: touropia.com/most-important-rivers-in-the-world

page 82: science360.gov/obj/video/95922d02-4fa0-43f9-81c1-393b2f704367/nature-strikes-flash-floods

page 89: youtube.com/watch?v=yFxO9yW3ls0

page 95: smokeybear.com/en/smokeys-history/story-of-smokey

page 95: youtube.com/watch?v=Myz93sXW66Y

page 100: kqed.org/news/11644927/eucalyptus-how-californias-most-hated-tree-took-root-2

page 105: youtube.com/watch?v=5hghT1W33cY

page 108: bbc.com/news/av/world-europe-40591756/
southern-italy-struck-by-wildfire

page 109: youtube.com/watch?v=t0LXCHCz62Y

SOURCE NOTES

Chapter One

1 Molesky, Mark. *This Gulf of Fire: The Great Lisbon Earthquake, or Apocalypse in the Age of Science and Reason.* Knopf, 2015.

2 Incorporated Research Institutions for Seismology. Education and Outreach Series, No. 3. www.iris.edu/hq/files/publications/brochures_onepagers/doc/EN_OnePager3.pdf

3 USGS Website. "Earthquake Magnitude, Energy Release, and Shaking Intensity." https://earthquake.usgs.gov/learn/topics/mag-intensity

Chapter Two

1 Oppenheimer, Clive. *Eruptions that Shook the World.* Cambridge University Press, 2011. pp. 355–363.

2 Abbott, Patrick L. *Natural Disasters.* McGraw-Hill, 2009. pp. 188–197.

3 Abbott, Patrick L. *Natural Disasters.* McGraw-Hill, 2009. pp. 188–197.

Chapter Three

1 Abbott, Patrick L. *Natural Disasters.* McGraw-Hill, 2009. pp. 42–44.

2 Abbott, Patrick L. *Natural Disasters.* McGraw-Hill, 2009. pp. 361–362.

3 Kerr, Jack. "Tropical Cyclone Mahina: Bid to have deadly March 1899 weather event upgraded in record books." Australian Broadcasting Corp, April 2, 2015.

Chapter Four

1 Annual Severe Weather Report Summary, 2018.

2 Abbott, Patrick L. *Natural Disasters.* McGraw-Hill, 2009. pp. 311–319.

Chapter Five

1 NASA Earth Observatory Website. "Mississippi River Sediment Plume." https://earthobservatory.nasa.gov/images/1257/mississippi-river-sediment-plume

2 Johnstown Area Heritage Association Website. "Statistics about the great disaster." https://www.jaha.org/attractions/johnstown-flood-museum/flood-history/facts-about-the-1889-flood

3 U.S. Census Bureau website. May 2019. https://www.census.gov/history/www/homepage_archive/2019/may_2019.html

4 *Earth Magazine*, "Dutch Masters: The Netherlands exports flood-control expertise."

Chapter Six

1 Abbott, Patrick L. *Natural Disasters.* McGraw-Hill, 2009. p 427.

2 USDA Natural Resources Conservation Services

3 Abbott, Patrick L. *Natural Disasters.* McGraw-Hill, 2009. p 433.

INDEX

INDEX

tornadoes and, 62–63
volcanic particles
    removed by, 36
    wildfires and, 102, 103
rhyolitic magma, 33
Richter scale/Richter, Charles, 16
Ring of Fire, 18, 29
rivers, vii, 2, 10, 20, 74–88
Russia, natural disasters in, 6, 82

S

Saffir-Simpson Hurricane
    Wind Scale, 53
scientific method, 6
sediment, 77–78, 80
seismographs, vi, 12,
    16–17, 20, 51
snow, 74, 77, 79, 83, 85
Songhua River, 80
space disasters, 6
storm surges, vi–vii, 4, 42, 48,
    53, 55. See also tsunamis
Syria, natural disasters in, vi

T

tectonic plates, 10, 14–15,
    18, 20, 27–29, 39
Teisserenc de Bort, Leon, vii
Texas, natural disasters in,
    vii, 48, 54–55, 105
Thailand, natural disasters
    in, vii, 23
thunderstorms
    floods and, 81, 82, 84
    hurricanes and, 43, 49, 51–52
    tornadoes and, 62–64, 68–69
    wildfires and, 98, 105
topography, 104–105
tornadoes
    effects of, vii, 3, 60–61,
        63, 65, 67–68
    of fire, 106
    forecasting and detection
        of, 68–70

formation of, 62–63
historically significant, 60–61
hurricanes spawning, 49
location of, 61–62, 63, 64
number and frequency
    of, 63, 64
paths of, 67
properties and characteristics
    of, 65–66
scale measuring
    intensity of, 66–67
shapes and sizes of, 65
sheltering and protection
    from, 70–71
tsunamis. See also storm surges
    earthquakes and, vi–vii, 10,
        11, 12, 16, 20–21, 23
    volcanoes and, vi, 26–27, 35

V

Virginia, natural disasters in, 68
volcanoes
    damage from, 34–38
    earthquakes, tectonic plates,
        and, 27–30, 35, 37, 39
    eruptions of, vi, 2, 3,
        26–27, 30–38
    forecasting and tracking
        of, 36–37, 40
    formation and location
        of, 28–30
    magma and, vi, 30–34, 37
    parts of, 34
    tsunamis and, vi, 26–27, 35
Volga River, 76

W

Washington, natural
    disasters in, 34
water, 2, 31, 45–46, 50, 100.
    See also floods; rain; rivers;
    storm surges; tsunamis
water cycle, 77

weather balloons, vii, 68
weather patterns. See also
    meteorological disasters
    volcanic eruptions affecting,
        26, 35–36, 38
    wildfires and, 92, 99, 102–104
Wegener, Alfred, vii
wildfires
    characteristics and
        personality of, 105–107
    classification of, 6
    control of, vii, 93–94, 95, 109
    effects of, vii, 3, 92–94,
        96, 99, 105–107
    fire-dependent ecosystems,
        vii, 94–96
    fuel for, 98, 99–101, 103
    as photosynthesis in
        reverse, 97
    prevention of, 106–107
    requirements for, 97–99
    sparks starting, 98, 105, 106
    spread of, 99
    surviving, 97
    topography affecting, 104–105
    weather, wind, and, 92,
        99, 102–105, 106
wind
    Foehn, 103–104
    hurricanes and, 4, 42,
        44–45, 47–56
    measuring of, 53, 58
    tornadoes, vii, 3, 49, 59–72
    wildfires and, 102–105, 106
Wisconsin, natural
    disasters in, 106

Y

Yangtze River, 74–75, 76
Yukon River, 83